something special
Seasonal and festive art and craft for children

Written and illustrated by Lyn Gray

First published in 1990 by
BELAIR PUBLICATIONS LIMITED
P.O. Box 12, Twickenham, England, TW1 2QL

© Lyn Gray

Series Editor Robyn Gordon
Designed by Richard Souper
Photography by Kelvin Freeman
Typesetting by Florencetype Ltd
Printed and bound by Heanor Gate Printing Limited

ISBN 0 947882 14 6

Acknowledgements

The author and publishers would like to thank the children of Orleans Infants School, Twickenham, Richmond-upon-Thames, for their hard work, both in termtime and holidays.

They would also like to thank Barbara Hume and Faith Morgan for their kind co-operation, and Meryl Gray (age 5) for the cover artwork.

Contents

Introduction

The school calendar contains many festivals and 'red letter' days. Each year teachers are expected to think of fresh ideas to celebrate these annual events. *Something Special* is compiled with a view to enlarging the fund of ideas that teachers may draw upon.

Some of the projects will be familiar, and are included to jog the reader's memory of old favourites; some are based on familiar themes but with an extra element added to make them more relevant to a classroom; some use familiar techniques which have been adapted for a particular occasion; others contain ideas which I hope are totally new to the readers.

Throughout the book precise instructions and measurements are given. There are times in a busy term when such help may be required; however, it is also hoped that teachers will regard the visual work as a springboard to stimulate their own ideas.

There is plenty of room for adaptation. It may well be that some of the photographed displays involve more preparation time and materials than are available, so necessitating simplification. Schools encompassing a broader range of cross-cultural festivals will need to adapt projects to their particular celebrations. Waste materials from local manufacturers are sometimes available to schools, and this can also direct craftwork in the classroom.

Each teacher knows the capabilities of the children in his/her class. Most of the projects are suitable for an infant school. Working with very young children, however, tends to require more preparation. Directions state if an idea is aimed at an older child, in which case top infants or lower juniors would best be involved.

Finally, it is hoped that the book provides fun and a few surprises for the children **and** the parents – who are often presented with the finished treasures. That sticky cardboard box may take pride of place on the mantelpiece and be admired for months.

Lyn Gray

Paper plate portraits

This is a simple activity which will brighten a classroom at the beginning of term and give the opportunity for newcomers to get to know each other.

Materials required

Small paper plates

Selection of paper giving variety of skin tones

White school glue

Chalks/crayons/felt-tip pens

Felt/wool/ribbon etc for decoration

Prepare paper by dividing sheets into strips which should be approx. 13cm × 70cm.

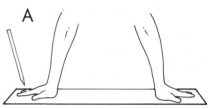

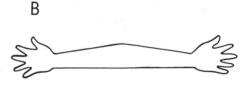

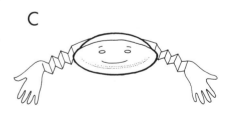

The children are divided into pairs, and then sit opposite their partners in order to draw a likeness. Each child takes a strip of paper which best matches the skin of his/her partner. Circles of similar paper may be stuck to the plate to give face colour (see photograph). Each child draws round his partner's hands, placed with fingers pointing outwards at either ends of the chosen strip of paper (see Fig A). The hand shapes are linked together with drawn lines and cut out (see Fig B). Portraits are drawn and decorated on each plate. The hand strips are then glued on to the back of the completed plate and pressed firmly into a concertina (see Fig C).

The finished portraits may be displayed on a board, or, by linking hands, they can form an effective frieze round the room. A more elaborate display could be achieved by first creating a long wall from chalk rubbings of brickwork. The plates would then be positioned as though the children were hanging over the wall (see Fig D).

Autumn hibernation

These two pages suggest a way of mounting a display on hibernation. It can be as simple or as elaborate as time permits. Ideally the project should begin with an outing to a park where the children can start collecting as many autumn fruits, leaves and seeds as possible. Our display included acorns, conkers, beech nuts, various fir cones, pine needles, sycamore seeds, grasses and leaves. These items were combined with vegetables and paper to depict hibernating animals.

Materials required for Hedgehog

Large fir cone	Pine needles
2 small acorns	Blu-Tack/Plasticine
5 beech nut cases	White school glue

Using small pieces of Plasticine or Blu-Tack, fix four beech nut cases under the fir cone to represent the hedgehog's feet; one beech nut case for the nose, and two small acorns for the eyes. Dip the stalk end of the pine needles into glue and then insert between fir cone scales (see Fig A). Continue until body is covered.

Materials required for Tortoise

Small fir cone	Brown and yellow pens
Pieces from large fir cone	Staples/glue
Brown paper	Blu-Tack/Plasticine

Cut a circle 16cm diameter from brown paper. Make four cuts towards centre (see Fig B) and decorate using brown and yellow pens. Overlap (see Fig C) to create shell shape, fixing with either glue or staples. Create head and forelegs using fir cone and fir cone pieces joined by Plasticine or Blu-Tack. Rest shell on top.

Materials required for Snake

Brown paper	Blu-Tack/Plasticine
Pens	2 small acorns
2 small acorns	White school glue
Leaves	

Cut a circle 20cm diameter from brown paper; draw and cut a spiral with the snake's head at centre (see Fig D). Decorate with pattern using leaves and pens. Complete with forked tongue and small acorn eyes attached with Blu-Tack or Plasticine.

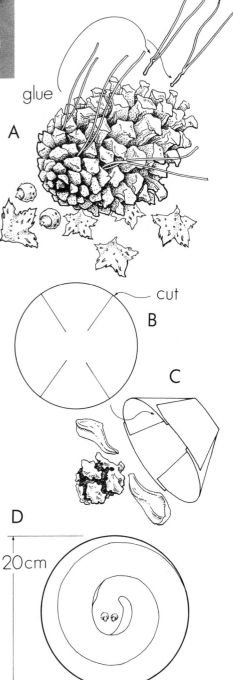

glue

A

cut

B

C

D

20cm

Materials required for Frog and Toad

Large potato
Brown paper
Circular adhesive labels
Brown pens

Eucalyptus fruits/poppy seed heads
Blu-Tack

Using Fig E as a guide, draw and cut two legs and two arms for each frog. Cut base off potato so that the frog is sitting in an upright forward position (see Fig F). Place eyes, arms and legs as in Fig F using Blu-Tack. Complete frog by drawing mouth and, in the case of toads, decorate with brown adhesive labels for warts.

Materials required for Dormouse

Small fir cone
String
Pink paper

Feathery grass seed head
White school glue

Cut dormouse ears from pink paper and insert near base of cone (see Fig G). Glue grass seed head onto length of string attaching the other end into pointed tip of cone. Dip stalk ends of the grass seed heads into glue and insert between cone scales. Cover body.

Materials required for Ladybird

Conker
Large and small circular self-adhesive labels (or paper and white school glue)

Black and red pens

Colour large label red with black head (see Fig H). Make cut along body to divide into two wings. Add the required number of black spots and cover conker with label.

To assemble display, paint a variety of boxes with dark autumnal colours. Staple securely onto background adding plastic flower pots for extra hibernating holes. Some boxes might have lids which open to reveal sleeping animals. Place all the animals into the display. Camouflage and decorate with autumn leaves.

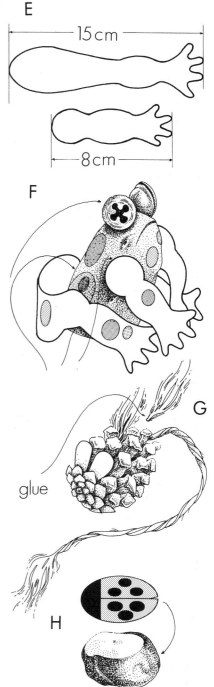

E

15 cm

8 cm

F

G

glue

H

Harvest Baskets

Apple tree baskets

Materials required

Florets of broccoli (or cauliflower)
White paper for covering
Green and red paint
White school glue

Tissue/crêpe paper for lining basket
Dowel
A small cardboard box

Help will be required to cover basket. The easiest method is to place the container in the centre of a sheet of paper marking round the bottom onto the paper. Turning the box on to its side, mark the shape again onto the paper. Repeat for all four sides allowing extra for overlapping at the corners and top (see Fig A). Cut round shape and apply glue to overlapping areas. Fix to basket.

Carefully cut florets in half ensuring the 'branches' are complete. Experiment with several to find florets which look most like trees. Brush green paint onto cut surface and either print directly onto the basket or more cautiously onto a strip of white paper which is then applied afterwards. The apples are printed using thin dowel dipped into red paint. The handle of the basket in the photograph was covered and then printed with a smaller floret to continue the apple tree design. Line and pad basket with crêpe or tissue paper.

Corrugated card basket

These are very simple and surprisingly effective, provided that square pieces are cut accurately.

Materials required

A small cardboard box
Corrugated card
White school glue

White tissue/doilies for lining basket

Using a template, cut the corrugated card into 4cm squares following the corrugations. These are then glued directly on to the sides of the container alternating the direction of the lines (see Fig B). Squares will have to be trimmed at the sides and bottom. Cover the handle and line basket with tissue and doilies as in photograph above.

The basic container can be a mushroom basket or a small strong cardboard box.

A

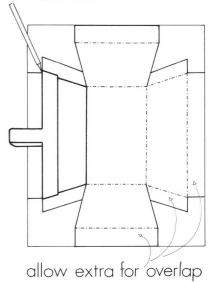

mark four sides

allow extra for overlap

B

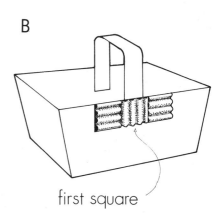

first square

Floral collage baskets

Materials required

Blue paper for covering
Green paper
Patterned paper (wallpaper, gift wrap, fabric catalogue)

Straws
White school glue
Tissue/crêpe for lining basket
A small cardboard box

First cover basket with blue paper (see instructions on previous page). Cut wavy green strip and glue round basket (see Fig C). Cut different sized circles and leaf shapes from patterned paper. Fold leaves along length. Glue shapes on to side of container to represent simple flowers using straws for stems (see Fig D). Glue only half of folded leaf onto basket so that they are three-dimensional. Cover handle with blue paper and line basket with tissue or crêpe paper.

Woven baskets

These baskets require rather more adult preparation work, but once done, four children can work on one basket, each weaving a side.

Materials required

Background paper of required colour
Strips of paper/ribbon/wool etc. of required colours

Adhesive or masking tape
White school glue
Tissue/crêpe for lining basket
A small cardboard box

Laying the basket on each of its sides, draw round each side on covering paper allowing extra width on long sides for overlapping corners (see Fig E). Cut shapes out and, using a craft knife, cut vertical lines 3cm apart (see Fig F).

Weave strips of paper/ribbon/wool etc. in and out of paper slots taking care to alternate slots in each row. End of woven strips are fastened with adhesive or masking tape on back of woven surface (see Fig G). When weaving is complete apply glue to overlapping parts and attach the two long sides to container, followed by the two short sides. Cover and decorate handle. Line basket with tissue or crêpe paper.

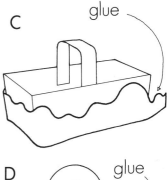

C — glue

D — glue

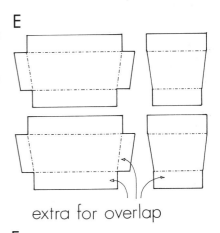

E

extra for overlap

F

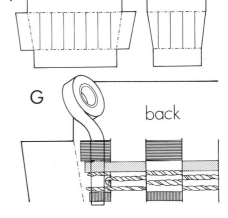

G

back

Hallowe'en Hats

Basic witch's hat

Materials required

Card for template – optional
Black paper

Glue/double sided adhesive tape/
staples

If several hats are to be produced, it is worth making a card template so that the children are able to draw and cut their own hats. The shape is a quarter segment of a circle radius 40cm. This may be drawn on to the card by placing one end of a tape measure at the centre of circle and swinging round other end, marking arc at 40cm point in tape (see Fig A). Cut template ready for children to draft and cut their hats.

Measure hats round individual heads to mark size. The children will then need assistance to form and glue hat with sharp point at top. It may help to roll point between fingers before gluing. A staple can be added to make joint stronger. Always use staples with smooth metal face on inside of hat otherwise hair may catch on staple ends.

Witch-on-a-broomstick

These figures fit on top of basic hat. However they may be used in other ways – the children can slip their fore finger through the pipe cleaner loop and use the witch as a type of finger puppet.

Materials required

Black paper
Black crêpe paper
Pipe cleaner
White craft ball
Drinking straw
Black cotton
Pens
White school glue

Glue end of pipe cleaner into bottom of craft ball to form neck. Make loop in pipe cleaner, twisting back round neck and leaving end pointing downwards (see Fig B). Using pens draw witch's face on to ball and colour the drinking straw black. Cut a piece of black paper approx. 3cm × 6cm. Fringe, and glue round bottom of straw (see Fig C). Apply glue to bottom of pipe cleaner and fit straw over it. Cut a piece of black crêpe 16cm × 30cm (see Fig D). Gather up and bind tightly round witch's neck allowing 5cm of the crêpe paper to stand up for collar (see Fig E).

Cut a circle diameter 14cm from the black paper. One quarter will make the pointed part of hat (see Fig F).

Cut a second circle diameter 8cm for brim. Fold in half and make cut, then repeat making cut in opposite direction (see Fig G). Push pointed section through cross cut in circle, and glue (see Fig H). Glue on to head. Bend head and neck back.

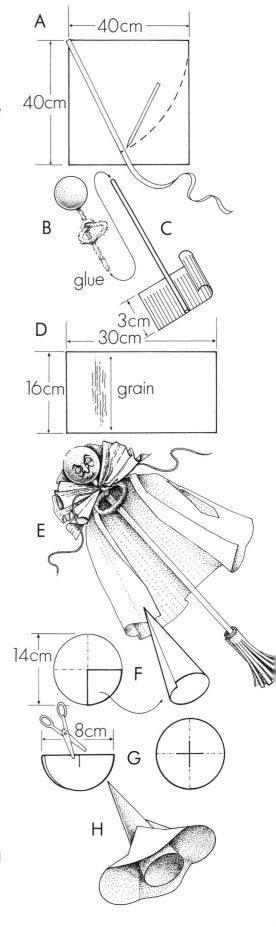

Wizard's hat

Materials required

Black paper
Yellow card
Black cotton

Invisible matt adhesive tape
Glue/double sided adhesive tape/staples

Draw and cut hat as for basic witch's hat. Do *not* make up. Cut three stars and moons preferably of varying sizes out of yellow card. Using the invisible tape attach 14cm lengths of black cotton to each. These are then taped to the hat with the smaller stars and moons nearer the point of the hat (see Fig I). Older children could thread cotton through a needle and stab thread through to back of paper securing them with tape. This makes a neater hat though it is impractical for very young children. Make up finished hat as for basic witch's hat.

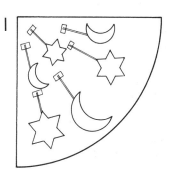

Witch's cat hat

Materials required

Card for template – optional
Black paper
White paper
Labels – optional

Pens
Glue/double sided adhesive tape/staples

If using templates, see previous page for basic witch's hat.
The template for the cat's head is based on a circle diameter 14cm placed over a triangle (see Fig J). Round off the tops of the ears. The template for the tail is based on a circle diameter 20cm which is then developed into a spiral shape (see Fig K).

Draw and cut basic witch's hat. Do *not* make up. Using the head template draw and cut cat's head allowing for 'furry' outline (see Fig L). Decorate head with labels, paper and pens. Whiskers may be made from narrow strips of white paper length 20cm. These are bent in half and glued on to face. When complete, staple cat's head to flat hat (see Fig L).

Make up hat as for basic witch's hat.

Stretch tail spiral over ruler to enable tail to hang well. Staple straight end to inside back of hat.

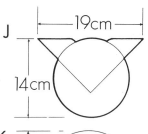

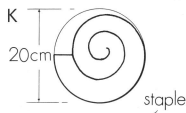

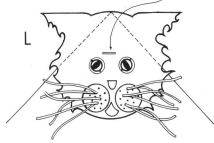

Hallowe'en spiders

This spider may be suspended by thread or perhaps fixed to a witch's hat.

Materials required

Thin card

Black wool

Black paper

Paper/adhesive labels for eyes

White school glue

Each spider requires two circles of card diameter 5cm. An adult will need to cut a further circle diameter 2cm from the centre of each (see Fig A). Prepare wool by cutting into lengths approx. 100cm. The children will make a pompom in the usual way by threading lengths of wool through both circles until the centre hole is filled (see Fig B). A wool needle will help in the finishing stages. Cut round circle edge (see Fig C). Separate the two card circles and tie a length of wool tightly between them, making a loop with the ends if spider is to be suspended (see Fig D). Cut card away and roll pompom between hands to obtain ball shape. Trim if necessary.

Cut strips of black paper 45cm × 1cm. Find centre of each strip and pleat fold from either end (see Fig E). Glue four pleated strips as in Fig F and glue underneath pompom. Complete spider with eyes, preferably red and black.

A

B   C

D

E

F

glue to bottom of pompom

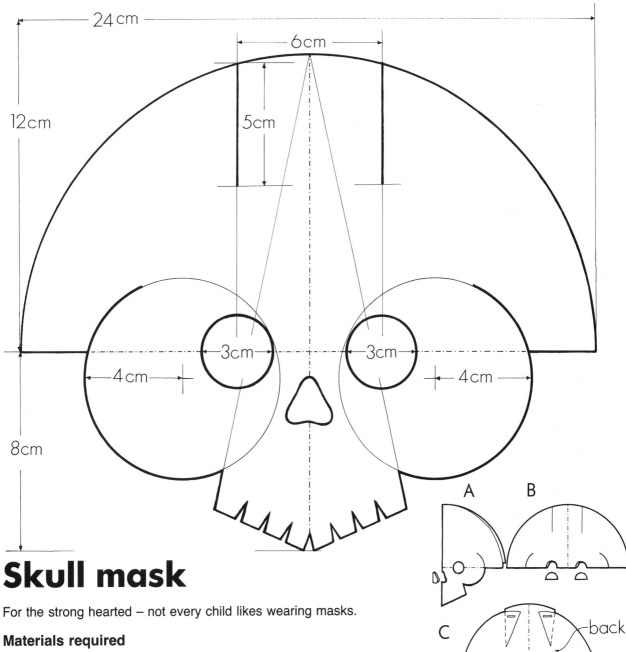

Skull mask

For the strong hearted – not every child likes wearing masks.

Materials required
Card for template
White paper
Staples

An adult will need to draw and cut a template using the card. The heavy outline in the large diagram is the cutting line. Measurements and folding lines are shown by a thinner line. Once the template is prepared, the children place it on to the white paper and draw round it carefully including eyes, nose, cheekbone and forehead lines. The mask can then be cut out. Fold as in Fig A to cut nose. Fold as in Fig B to cut eyes. Open mask up and overlap the two forehead cuts as in Fig C. Staple in position so that the smooth side of the staple is next to the child's face.

Cut head bands from white paper approx. 4cm × 60cm. Fit to each child's head and secure ends together with staple, whilst child is wearing headband. Hold mask in correct position over face and mark join on headband (see Fig D). Remove from child and staple into position, again making sure that the smooth side of the metal is next to the child's hair.

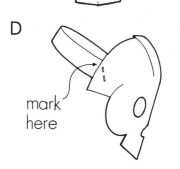

GUY FAWKES

Rocket mobile

Materials required

Variety of cardboard tubes (eg. toilet roll tubes, kitchen paper tubes, sweet containers and tubes from rolls of fabric)

Black paper

Thin card

Fluorescent paint

Sequins or foil scraps

White school glue

Invisible adhesive tape

Thread

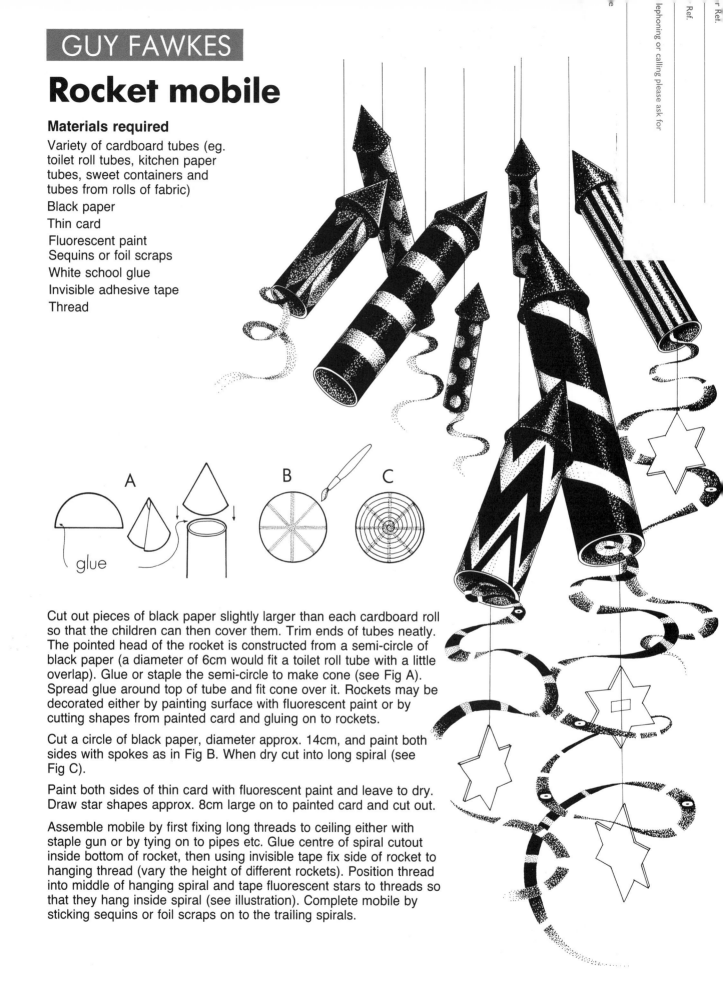

Cut out pieces of black paper slightly larger than each cardboard roll so that the children can then cover them. Trim ends of tubes neatly. The pointed head of the rocket is constructed from a semi-circle of black paper (a diameter of 6cm would fit a toilet roll tube with a little overlap). Glue or staple the semi-circle to make cone (see Fig A). Spread glue around top of tube and fit cone over it. Rockets may be decorated either by painting surface with fluorescent paint or by cutting shapes from painted card and gluing on to rockets.

Cut a circle of black paper, diameter approx. 14cm, and paint both sides with spokes as in Fig B. When dry cut into long spiral (see Fig C).

Paint both sides of thin card with fluorescent paint and leave to dry. Draw star shapes approx. 8cm large on to painted card and cut out.

Assemble mobile by first fixing long threads to ceiling either with staple gun or by tying on to pipes etc. Glue centre of spiral cutout inside bottom of rocket, then using invisible tape fix side of rocket to hanging thread (vary the height of different rockets). Position thread into middle of hanging spiral and tape fluorescent stars to threads so that they hang inside spiral (see illustration). Complete mobile by sticking sequins or foil scraps on to the trailing spirals.

Star and cracker chain

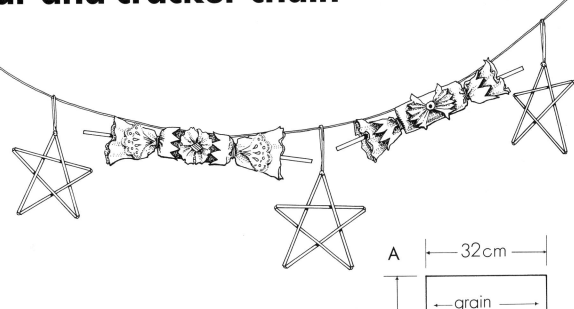

Materials required for Crackers

Toilet roll tubes

Bright crêpe paper

Long art straws

Doilies, foil, crêpe or sweet
papers for decoration

Thin thread

White school glue

Adhesive tape

Each cracker requires a piece of crêpe paper approx. 32cm × 28cm
with grain as in Fig A. Wrap crêpe round toilet roll tube with the grain
running lengthways. Push straw through tube and lightly bind both
ends of toilet roll with thread (see Fig B). Gently stretch crêpe ends of
cracker. Decorate as wished. Pleated fans and circles of crêpe paper
can look attractive (see Fig C).

Materials required for Straw Stars

Five plastic straws

Thin stiff string or raffia

Cut piece of string or raffia the length of seven straws. Thread through
the five straws and knot at either end (see Fig D). Construct five-point
star by following Fig E-G. Knot two ends together and adjust shape to
make even star shape.

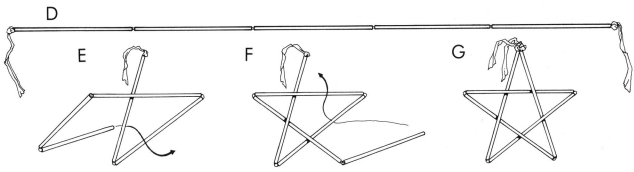

Assemble chain by attaching crackers to thread with adhesive tape.
Suspend stars in between. Paper clips or Blu-Tack can be used to
prevent suspended stars from sliding along the chain.

Stars can be a useful decoration, the more so as Christmas approaches. On the next few pages are reminders of some of the different methods of making stars, not forgetting the straw star on the previous page.

Two-dimensional 6-point star

This is a simple method of drafting a star either by an adult to make templates, or by children old enough to use a compass.

With the use of the compass, draw a circle the size of the required star. Keeping the angle of the open compass constant, place the metal point on the circumference of the circle and make a small arc either side across the circumference (see Fig A). Moving the metal point round to one of these arcs continue to make further arcs (see Fig B). The circumference should divide into six equal parts which are then joined as in Fig C making a 6-point star comprising two equilateral triangles.

Pleated star

Using thin paper or tissue cut a rectangle at least three times longer than its width. Pleat-fold carefully (see fig D). Press edges with finger nail. Secure centre with paper clip, staple, elastic band or thread and cut off two corners diagonally (see Fig E). Pull sides down and glue (see Fig F).

If graph paper is used, the lines will help the children to make parallel fold lines and, by colouring symmetric strips across the paper before folding (see Fig G), the finished star can be very decorative.

Paper strip star

Stars can be made from long narrow pieces of paper. A strip 1cm × 40cm will make a tiny star; a length from a roll of cash register paper 6cm × 250cm will make a larger one. Find the centre of the length of paper and fold at that point to make a right angle (see Fig H). Keep folding strips across each other alternatively (see Figs I and J). Continue until all the paper is used. You now have a fold as in Fig K. Curve round and secure ends together (see Fig L).

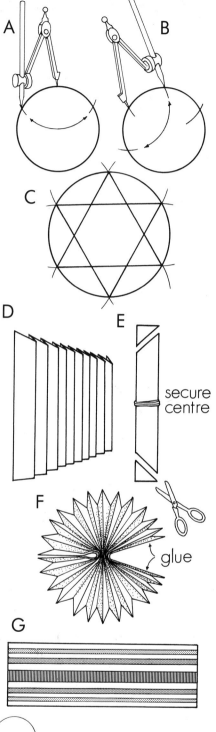

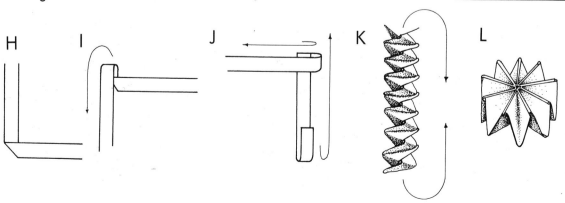

Cut and fold stars

These stars are very quick and easy to make. The finished result will depend on the shape of the paper used and how it is cut and folded – it is worth experimenting. The designs can be developed into simple cards either by mounting onto a different coloured background or by placing over a cut out window so that the light can shine through.

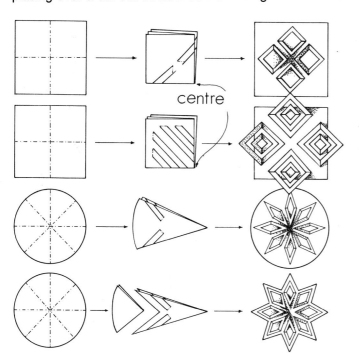

Cone stars

Star shapes can be constructed from a number of cones. Each cone is made from a square of paper. Diagonal corners are raised and glued across each other forming a point at the base (see Fig A and B). Care needs to be taken to obtain a good point – very young children will find this difficult. A simple star shape will require twelve cones glued onto a base (see Fig C). With some experimenting other patterns can be produced and, by varying the size of the cones, more elaborate designs are possible (see Fig D and E). By working in groups large scale stars can be produced.

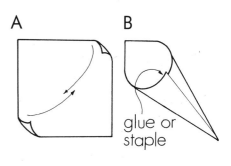

A   B

glue or staple

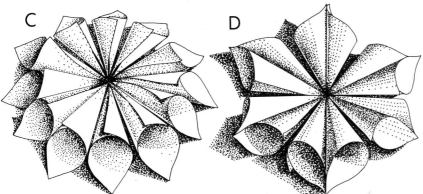

C   D

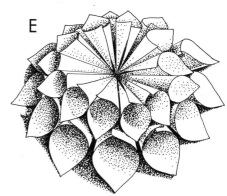

E

Christmas decorations

These designs continue the theme of stars but broaden it out into general Christmas decorations. Strips of paper approx. 1cm wide and white school glue are all that are required (a paper guillotine will produce strips quickly). Gummed brown paper bought for wrapping parcels could also be used; and, for a more lasting decoration, strips of woven straw sold in craft shops make an attractive though more expensive alternative. By curving and bending the strips, the children can practise making simple shapes (see Fig A).

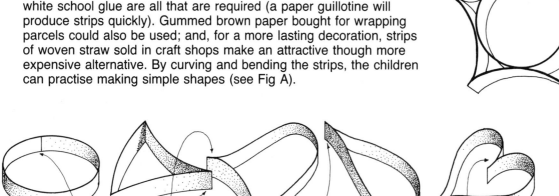

glue   glue

They should be encouraged to use the glue sparingly applying it with a cocktail stick rather than a spatula to ensure joints dry quickly.
By combining shapes of different sizes, elaborate designs can evolve.
The completed decorations may be suspended from the ceiling.

18

Printed Christmas tree card

Materials required

Scraps of balsa wood and pencil ends for printing

Mid tone paper

Paints – preferably including one fluorescent colour

By printing with just three different shapes (see Fig A) the children can experiment in making Christmas tree designs. These may then be mounted to make cards or printed on a long strip of paper to decorate the classroom with a Christmas forest frieze.

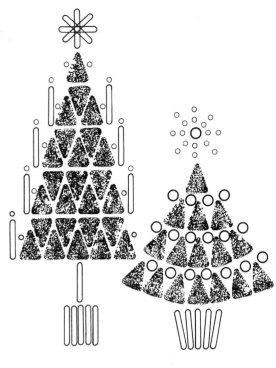

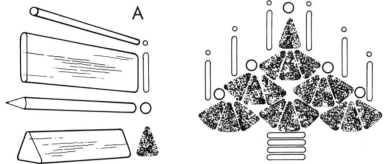

A

Father Christmas face card

Directions are given for a particular face; however the construction is useful for any design in which a 3-dimensional effect is sought.

Materials required

Thin card (black looks attractive)

White terylene wadding sold by the yard for quilting

Adhesive labels/coloured paper

Pink felt – optional

White school glue

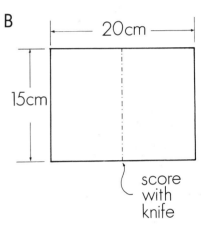

B

20cm

15cm

score with knife

Cut a piece of card approx. 15cm × 20cm, and score down centre (see Fig B). Fold card in half and draw two parallel lines 3cm apart and 4.5cm long in middle of folded length (see Fig C). Cut along drawn lines and open card. Score two lines joining the two cut lines (see Fig D). Shut card, pushing centre strip forward (see Fig E).

The children assemble Father Christmas's face. From the wadding cut a circle 12cm diameter for the face, a circle 9cm diameter for the beard, and a circle 5cm diameter for bobble on hat. Using coloured paper, adhesive labels and felt, complete the face. When finished, glue centre of the back of face on to projecting strip. If cards are to be taken home it is advisable to put them in envelopes.

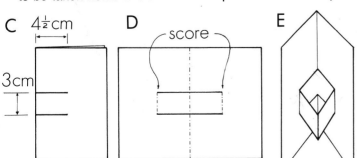

C

4½cm

3cm

D

score

E

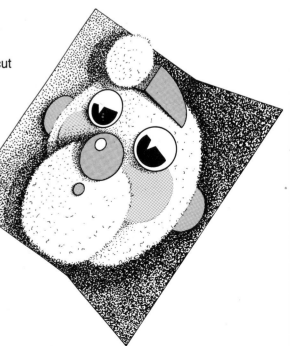

Christmas pudding card

This is a pudding that smells delicious.

Materials required

White card
White paper
Dark paper
Green paper
Red adhesive labels/paper

White school glue
Pudding mix to include:
Brown sugar/sand/oats/raisins/
seeds/mixed spice/whole cloves

A piece of white card should be cut 30cm × 16cm. Score down centre. Using circular object draw two circles 15cm diameter in both halves (see Fig A). Fold card in half and cut top of circles off (see Fig B). Apply glue thickly on to front circle and press in pudding mix. Glue larger raisins, cloves etc individually. Leave to dry and shake excess mixture off. Cut and glue base from dark paper and icing from white paper using circular object for guide. Complete pudding with cut out paper holly leaves and red berry labels.

helpful to study real holly leaves

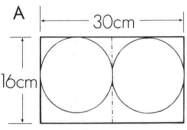

A

30cm

16cm

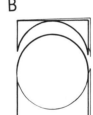

B

Christmas cracker card

Materials required

Thick coloured paper
Bright paper/adhesive labels/
ribbon for decorating

Straws
White school glue

Cut strip from thick paper 50cm × 10cm. Lightly mark the strip into eight equal parts (see Fig C). Fold card as in Fig D and shape ends of cracker. Reverse and glue straws to project beyond card as in Fig E. Decorate cracker with bright papers, labels and ribbon. A Christmas message or joke could be written on white paper and glued inside to be revealed when the card is opened. Younger children might like to draw presents and party hats.

C

50cm

10cm

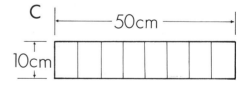

D

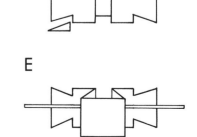

E

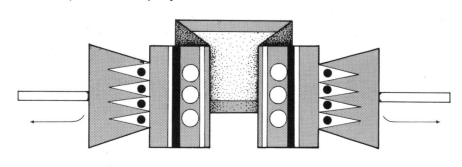

Father Christmas beard card

A

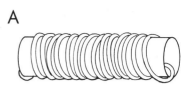

Materials required

Thick black paper	White paper
Tubular object	Thin sponge – optional
String	Coloured paper
Pipe cleaner	Pens

B

Experiment printing on rough paper:

Wrap string round tubular object allowing space between each circumference (see Fig A), secure ends with tape. Either roll over a thin sponge saturated in white paint or apply paint directly on to string using paint brush. Then experiment twisting, rolling and dragging tube on rough paper to print Father Christmas's hair and beard. Tight curls can be printed from a shaped pipe cleaner (see Fig B).

Now the card:

Cut length of black paper three times its width. Fold into three as in illustration. On the top square make a simple collage face with hat. Open card out, and by printing with white paint create a hairy Father Christmas. Perhaps he has a few robins and Christmas mice living in his beard?

Pleated Christmas tree card

Materials required

Bright coloured papers including green	Adhesive labels
Lolly sticks	White school glue

For basic card use piece of paper approx. 60cm × 45cm and fold as in Fig C to provide strong backing. Glue two lolly sticks on front of card for tree trunk (see Fig D). Using green paper, cut a triangle height 30cm, base 20cm (see Fig E). Fold into pleats approx. 2cm wide. Stick carefully on to card by applying glue top and bottom and behind ridge of pleats. Cut piece of coloured paper for flower pot approx. 5cm x 9cm. Glue over lolly sticks, raising centre to give three dimensional effect. Cut strips of paper and pleat to form decorations and star. Apply glue sparingly. Complete design with adhesive labels.

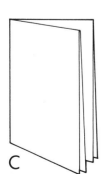

C

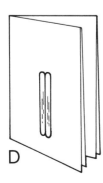

D

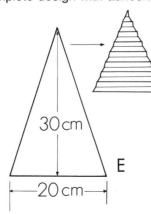

E

30cm

20cm

Father Christmas calendar

The commercial Advent calendar has 24 windows to open prior to Christmas; this poses a problem for the classroom in that term finishes before December 24, and if every child is to contribute to the calendar more windows are likely to be required. One solution is to have a window for each child and to start opening them in November.

We used a wax crayon rubbing of brickwork for our chimneys but the bricks could be printed with pieces of polystyrene or stencilled through card equally successfully.

Materials required

White paper – thin but not transparent	Coloured paper for Father Christmas and chimney pots
Masking tape	Adhesive labels
Blue wax crayon	Thick white paint for snowflakes
Blue background paper	White school glue

Find a wall with recessed pointing if possible. Secure pieces of white paper to brickwork with masking tape. Rub hard over surface with a wax crayon emphasising edges of the individual bricks. Continue until the brickwork shows clearly.

Piece together sheets of rubbings to obtain chimney shapes, taping joins at back. Cut profile of chimney shapes (see Fig A). The required number of 'doors' can then be cut into the brickwork by an adult using a sharp knife. Leave fourth side uncut as hinge (see Fig A).

Each child is given a piece of paper slightly larger than the opening on which to draw a Christmas picture. Glue is applied round the edge of the pictures which are fixed behind the openings. The brick covering the window is held closed with a numbered adhesive label.

Prepare the background. Our snowflakes were printed with lolly sticks, pencils and dowel (see Fig B). Glue chimneys on to background and decorate with Father Christmas and chimney pots. Remove numbered sticky labels to open windows which can be held back by using same label (see Fig C).

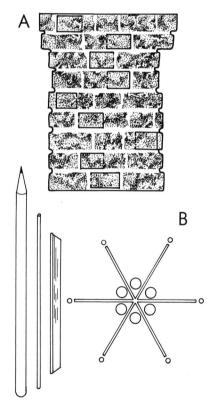

A

B

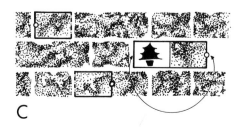

C

Christmas trees

How many different greens can you count on our Christmas trees?

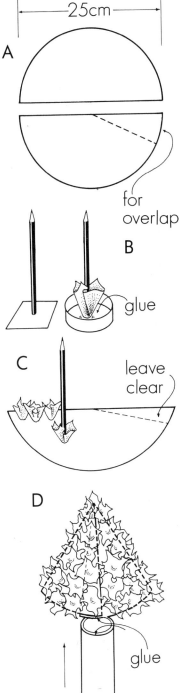

Materials required

Green paper
Red paper
Toilet roll tube
Tissue and crêpe paper in contrasting greens

Bright labels/sequins/glitter thread for decorating
White school glue

First prepare green tissue and crêpe paper by cutting it into quantities of 4cm squares.

Cover toilet tube with red paper. Fix with the minimum of glue, and trim ends.

Cut a circle diameter 25cm from the green paper. Fold circle and cut into two halves, each half forming the basis for a tree. Mark out a section of the semi-circle to be left free from tufting (see Fig A). Place a pencil end onto the centre of a tissue/crêpe square. Draw up paper round pencil and dip into glue (see Fig B). Position on to green base (see Fig C). Continue until all but marked section is covered with contrasting greens. Apply glue on to marked section and curve semi-circle round to make cone shape (see Fig D). Hold firmly until stuck. Untidy joins can always be hidden with extra tufting.

Apply glue round the edge of one end of the toilet tube and insert inside cone. When glue is dry decorate tree with labels, sequins and glitter thread, completing with angel or star if wished.

Flying angels

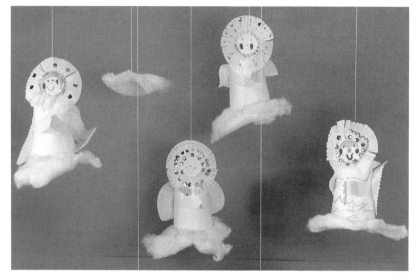

These angels are simple enough for very young children to make.

Materials required for each Angel

White paper cup
White paper cake cases
White paper
Large round white adhesive label
White school glue

Cotton wool
Pencils, pens, sequins for decoration
Elastic thread for hanging

Prepare each cup for hanging by knotting the end of a length of elastic thread and with the use of a large needle pulling it through the centre bottom of the cup (see Fig A). Using the white paper folded in half, cut arms 5cm in length with hand end placed on the fold (see Fig B). Draw face on an adhesive label and position in centre of a flattened cake case. Decorate with pencils, pens and sequins to resemble bright halo. Glue onto front of cup so that head projects above cup. Make wings out of halved paper cake case, draw hands on arms and glue both in required position. Flatten out a length of cotton wool until it is larger than the cup base. Apply glue to rim of cup and sit angel on top of it. Display with angels at different heights with additional clouds.

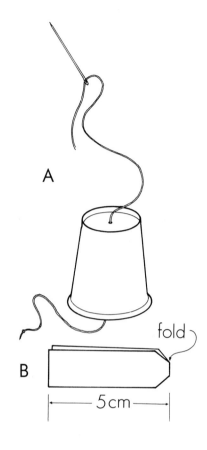

A

B fold

|← 5cm →|

Folded angel

This is a more intricate angel for older children who are able to use a compass. All that is required is paper, compass and pens. Follow dimensions given in Fig C. Decorate as Fig D. Cut along heavy line and fold as in Fig E.

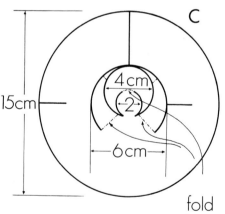

C

15cm

4cm

2

6cm

fold lines

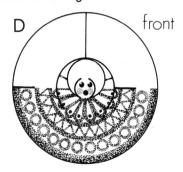

D   front

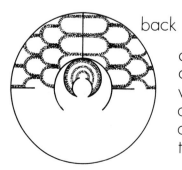

back

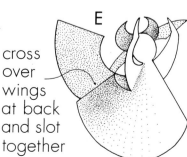

E

cross over wings at back and slot together

Christmas flock of sheep

There were shepherds keeping watch over their flock by night.

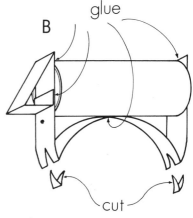

The shepherds in the photograph are similar to that shown on page 33 without spiderplant. Hair can be made from cotton wool or knitting wool and hats from folded paper cake cases.

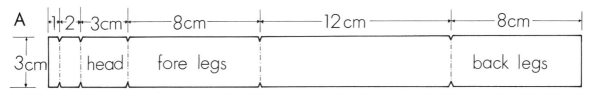

A |‑1‑|‑2‑|‑3cm‑|‑‑‑8cm‑‑‑|‑‑‑‑‑12cm‑‑‑‑‑|‑‑‑8cm‑‑‑|

3cm : head : fore legs : back legs

Materials required for one Sheep

Card for template – optional
Toilet roll tube
Black/white thick paper
Black and pink pens

White/beige/cream wool/string/raffia/tissue/ribbon etc
White school glue

If several children are making sheep it is worth cutting a template so that the fold lines are marked on the strip used for the head and legs. Follow dimensions given in Fig A, and cut out of card. The children draw round the template on to the thick paper marking notches. The strip is then cut out and folded as in Fig B and glued on to toilet roll tube. Cut triangles out of strip to give leg shape as shown. Whilst drying, cut wool etc into 17cm lengths. The quickest method is to wind it round a card or book of the correct width and cut at either end (see Fig C). Apply glue along toilet roll and attach the pieces of thread. Trim ends, keeping the cuttings (see Fig D).

Using black paper cut one circle 5cm diameter for the head and two circles 4cm diameter for the horns. Glue wool trimmings on to head circle and apply sheep's face on top (see Fig E). Draw a spiral on to horn circles. Cut out and carefully pull centre forwards (see Fig F). Glue horns behind head and complete sheep by gluing on to body.

The basic construction of the sheep made from a toilet roll tube and a strip of paper can be adapted quite easily to most four legged animals.

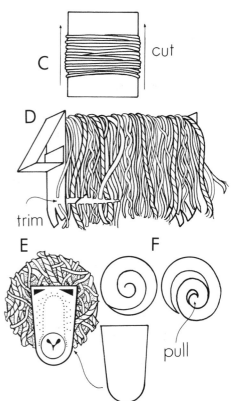

25

Sweet jar snowman

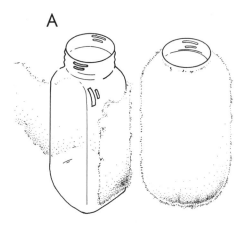

A

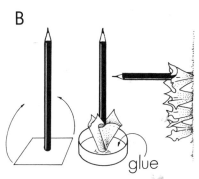

B

This snowman could contain small Christmas gifts to surprise the children on the last day of term.

Materials required

A large plastic sweet jar from a confectionery shop

A large roll of cotton wool

Newspaper

White crêpe paper

White tissue paper

Cardboard for base

Thin black card

Buttons, cotton, braid etc. for decoration

White school glue

Small groups of children can work on the body, base and head quite independently.

Body – Pad the jar to the required shape by wrapping cotton wool round it (see Fig A). Cut squares approx. 4cm of crêpe and tissue paper. Place pencil end on to centre of square. Draw up paper over pencil and dip into glue. Position on to body still using pencil (see Fig B). Cover all body except base.

C

leave clear

Base – Cut circle of cardboard approx. 50cm diameter. Place jar on centre and draw round. Spreading glue on to cardboard, tuft remaining area using balls of cotton wool with paper (see Fig C).

Head – Screw up sheets of newspaper to required size. Use white stretched crêpe for last layer securing with glue. Tuft with paper leaving area where head sits on sweet jar.

Hat – If possible find a round biscuit tin of required size for the children to use as a guide for cutting side, top and brim of hat from black card. Glue side join of hat followed by the brim and lastly the top (see Fig D).

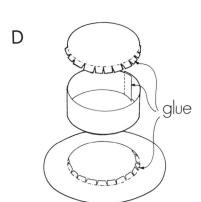

D

glue

Assemble snowman and decorate as wished. Snowballs can be suspended from the ceiling. Each is made from eight circles of tissue using the method described on page 44.

Frosted wall hanging

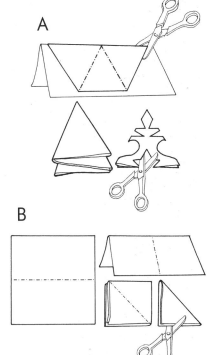

The frosted designs in the photos were glued on to a backing of semi-transparent calico which can look equally effective hung against a wall or window.

Materials required

White card	White straws
Thin white paper	Sugar lumps, sequins, glitter
Scraps of reflective papers eg. silver paper, foil, 'mother of pearl'	Semi-transparent fabric
	Dowelling
Paper doilies	Glue

Snowflakes

If possible these should have the correct six pointed star shape. Children can be helped by drawing three times round an equilateral triangle placed on the edge of a folded piece of thin white paper (see Fig A). Cut out shape and fold. Make decorative snips to produce flakes.

Younger children will find it easier to make a snowflake from a square piece of paper approx. 14cm folded into eighths as in Fig B.

Frosted Square Panels

Prepare squares of white card approx. 13cm. These may be decorated as a six pointed star shape or a four pointed star shape (see Fig C). Glue paper scraps, doilies, straws, sequins, sugar lumps etc. to make star design.

Wallhanging

Cut material to the desired length allowing an extra 5cm top and bottom for hem. Turn material under (as Fig D) and machine sew to provide slots for the dowelling in order to stretch hanging.

Glue squares and flakes on to the material after the dowelling has been inserted. An attractive pattern is achieved by alternating flakes and squares. If time is short mount directly on to mid tone or black paper.

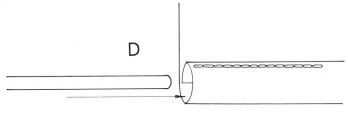

Toboggan and ski run

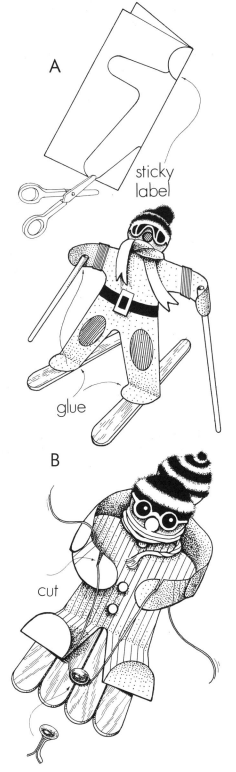

A seasonal display incorporating colours with use of ordinal numbers.

Materials required

White card

Coloured papers

White round adhesive labels

Lolly sticks

Cocktail sticks

Coloured straws

Coloured pencils and scraps for decorating figures

White school glue

Paper fasteners

Cardboard boxes

Stapler

Double sided adhesive tape

Figures

Prepare 15cm squares of coloured paper allowing at least three squares of each colour. Fold squares in half. Draw simple figure on to the fold using the full length of paper (see Fig A). A ginger bread man cutter could be used as a template. Use adhesive label for face. Cut out figures and decorate with pens, crayons and scraps of similar colour.

Toboggan

Cut rectangular paper base 10cm × 4cm and cover with four glued lolly sticks. Paper fasteners can be used to anchor string for figures to hold (see Fig B). Sit two figures on sledge. Glue in place. The third figure can be glued on to lolly stick skis using coloured straws for ski sticks.

Snow Slopes

Cover wall and table top with white paper. Create support for slopes with cut down boxes forming triangle against wall (see Fig C). Cut six strips of card approx. 13cm × 100cm. It may be necessary to join card for required length. Secure strips on to wall, support and table top creating different slopes with use of staples or double sided adhesive tape (see Figure C). Position each coloured team on a different slope.

A simple display can be mounted by drawing teams directly on to white paper strips, and fastened between wall and table top (see Fig D).

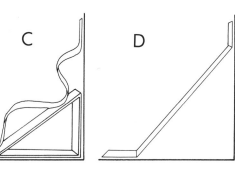

Get well card

A card designed to cheer an invalid – each patchwork square lifts to reveal a joke or, in the case of younger children, a comic drawing.

Materials required

Large sheet of thick paper approx. 65cm × 50cm

White crêpe paper

Scraps of patterned wallpaper/wrapping paper/plain paper and pens

Paper doilies – optional

Glue, or double sided adhesive tape

Measurements are given for a quilt of twenty-five squares. This may be enlarged depending on the number of children contributing. Fold card in half. Leaving a margin of 1.5cm round the bottom and sides, mark out rows of 6cm squares for patchwork quilt. Draw a second line 1cm below top of each square where glue or adhesive tape will be applied (see Fig A). At this stage each child chooses a square and writes a short joke or draws directly on to the card (writing has to be small). 6cm squares of wrapping paper (or plain squares decorated with pens by the children – graph paper would lend itself to geometric designs) are then fixed over the children's work, applying glue or tape in the space provided. Cut a piece of white crêpe 30cm × 30cm using pinking shears if possible and fold (see Fig B). Glue on to card to form the pillow and sheet. The pillow could be slightly padded and the sheet trimmed with paper doilies. Cut out collage portrait of invalid and slip between the sheets.

A

6cm

'Doctor doctor I think I'm a curtain'
'Well pull yourself together'

area for glue

B

Valentine jigsaw card

A

15cm

Materials required

Thin white card
Coloured pens
Envelopes

Each child will require a square piece of white card approx. 15cm × 15cm. With the use of a template, or freehand, draw a heart in the square. Using coloured pens, decorate the heart with bands of patterns until the shape is covered (see Fig A). Turn the card over and mark out simple jigsaw shapes (see Fig B). The child's skill with scissors will dictate how simple the shapes need to be. Cut out. The jigsaw could be kept in an envelope marked 'Mend A Broken Heart'.

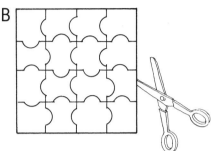

B

Chalked hearts card

Materials required

Thin card for heart templates
Paper
Coloured chalks

Prepare small heart shaped templates from squares of card 4cm × 4cm. The children can chalk heavily round the template and then smudge the line whilst still holding the heart in place (see Fig C).

C

Printed hearts card

Materials required

Potatoes
Paints
Paper

With the use of a potato print, children can experiment with the arrangement of hearts to create different patterns. Older children could concentrate on ones which leave interesting shapes between the heart prints. Mid-tone coloured paper, printed with bright paints can work well in this context. Attractive borders can be printed. Patterns can be combined with drawing; for example, the Queen of Hearts (see Fig D).

D

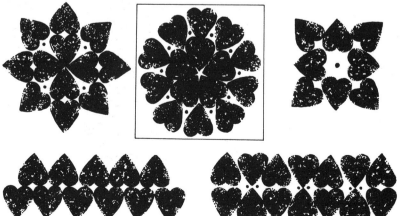

Valentine hearts mobile

These hanging hearts could be suspended in a line across the classroom or hung at varying heights in the corner of the room.

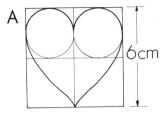

A

6cm

Materials required

White card for templates

White, pink or red paper (or combination of these)

Plastic straws

Ribbon or thread for loops

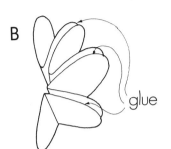

B

glue

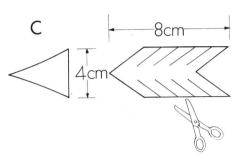

C

8cm

4cm

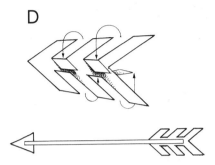

D

Prepare heart-shaped templates by drawing a 16cm square and marking it lightly into quarters (see Fig A). Draw two 8cm circles in the top half and complete heart shape by drawing symmetrical lines down to the centre bottom curving them in slightly above the point.

For each hanging heart, the children will need to cut eight heart shapes out of paper. Fold each in half and then glue four hearts together (see Fig B). Repeat for other half.

Cut point and feather for straw arrow out of paper (see Fig C). Make four cuts into the feather. Fold two strips towards you and two strips away from you (see Fig D). Make two cuts either end of straw and slot point and feather into them. Glue together the two halves of the heart, sandwiching and sticking the arrow and ribbon loop between them (see Fig E).

The three-dimensional heart can be easily adapted to a Valentine card. Prepare four heart shapes and glue together as for the hanging heart. Glue these inside a folded card (see Fig F).

F

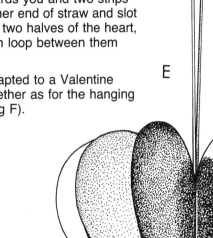

E

Cress gardener and wheelbarrow

This is a variation on the more usual method of growing cress in egg shells. The figure can of course be determined by the children. The illustration only gives one idea, which is probably more suitable for older children.

Materials required for Gardener Figure

Toilet roll tube

Polystyrene egg box

Cotton wool

Cress seeds

Stapler

Pink, green and brown paper

Dark plastic refuse bag

Pen and scraps for decoration

White school glue

Double sided adhesive tape

Cut up the bottom half of the egg box to provide suitable containers for the cotton wool. Staple one inside toilet roll tube (see Fig A). Cover roll with green paper fixing the back with glue or adhesive tape. Using pink paper for the head, green paper for the arms, plastic for the gloves and wellingtons, and brown paper for the apron, cut shapes using Fig B as a guide if required. Glue pieces on to body placing apron over wellingtons. Draw face and decorate with cotton wool, adhesive labels, etc. A coating of white glue over the head can stop pen marks from running when cress is watered. Fill container with moist cotton wool and sprinkle cress seed over it. Cover with paper until germination. Keep moist, watering carefully.

Materials required for Wheelbarrow

Small box, preferably a matchbox

Cotton wool

Hair grips

Coin/button

White school glue

Cut a strip off the matchbox cover to provide legs for the back of the wheelbarrow, glue to the bottom of the box (see Fig C). Cut a slot in the centre front of the box and insert coin/button for the wheel. Use two hair grips for handles. Fill with moist cotton wool and proceed as above.

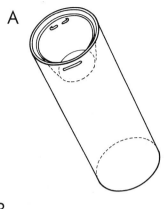

A

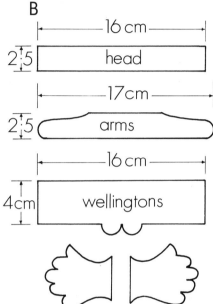

B

16 cm

2.5

head

17 cm

2.5

arms

16 cm

4 cm

wellingtons

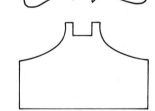

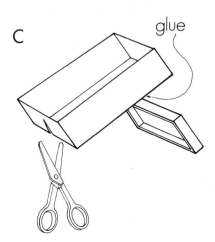

C

glue

32

Spider plant farmer

Materials required for Farmer Figure

Parent spider plant with small plantlets

Small plastic bag 21cm × 18cm (bought in rolls)

House plant compost

Toilet roll tube

Mixed papers

Pens, pipe cleaner and scraps for decoration

White school glue/double sided adhesive tape

Hairgrip

Create the figure as with the preceding gardener. If the illustrated smock is required, the piece of paper should be curved to obtain the flared shape (see Fig A). The crook is made from a pipe cleaner. Slide a plastic bag down the centre of the figure until the bottom reaches the bottom of the tube. Fold the top over the tube and fill the bag with house plant compost to 2cm below top. Moisten thoroughly. Cut spider plantlets off parent plant leaving some stalk. Using the hair grip peg plantlet down securely into soil (see Fig B). Trim plastic bag leaving 2cm above tube. This will help protect figure from watering which will need to be done carefully from a small jug. Keep very moist. Plantlets can eventually be transplanted into flower pots.

Monsters or mad professors would lend themselves to this project – or indeed a variety of faces (see Fig C).

C

Magic islands

Materials required

Carrots

Transplant plastic cartons

Paper and pens etc.

Either the children work together on a large piece of paper to produce an underwater seascape using collage and drawing, or each child is given a circle of paper approx. 20cm diameter to work on individual underwater scenes. Cut off 2cm from the top of each carrot and place in the carton with water reaching half way up the carrot (see illustration). Place on top of seascape in a light place.

keep watered and watch

33

Jack and the beanstalk display

It is possible to make a special display out of the germination of beans which are often planted during the spring and summer term.

Materials required for Germination

Small flower pots each with plastic container

Packet of runner beans

Planting compost

Thin string/strong cotton

Fill flower pots with a little compost. Plant two beans (for safety) at required depth and cover with compost. Dampen thoroughly and place on container to catch drainage. Position along light windowsill if possible. After germination provide a row of support strings secured firmly from under sill to top of window if that is practical.

Jack's House

Materials required

Paper

Coloured pens

Take a piece of paper approx. 20cm × 20cm. Fold in half and open. Fold two edges towards centre (see Fig A). Firm with nail. Turn over. Fold in half and open. Fold two edges towards centre (see Fig B). Press firmly with nail. Lift left and right top corners and reposition to obtain roof line (see Fig C). Turn over and decorate with pens. Open back and fit round flower pot (see Fig D).

Jack and his Mother

Children will need to be able to tie knots.

Materials required

Pieces of thick card approx. 10cm wide

Thick coloured wools

Pipe cleaners cut into 7cm lengths

Scraps, paper, felt, doilies etc. for decoration

White school glue

Wind wool round a piece of card approx. 30 times. Tie wool together securely at one end and cut the other end (see Fig E). Bind tightly at neck to make head. Knot securely (see Fig F). Thread length of pipe cleaner through body and bind tightly at waist. Knot securely (see Fig G). Divide wool into two legs below waist and bind tightly at ankles; knot securely (see Fig H). Decorate figures using scraps provided.

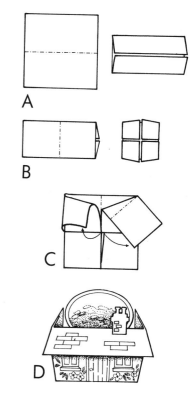

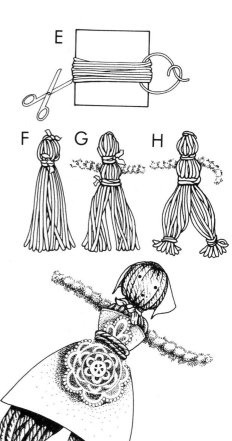

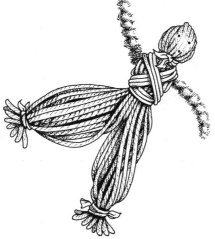

As the bean shoots climb up the support strings, Jack can climb the bean stalk. Fold pipe cleaner arms round stem above leaf joint. Clouds, sun and castle may be added as shoots grow higher. Perhaps shortly before display is to be dismantled, a giant boot could mysteriously appear from out of the clouds.

Water-lilies

Older children able to use a compass will find this lily easy. Young children could draw round circular objects of the right size starting with the largest circle so that they can centre the smaller ones.

Materials required

Thin paper
Compass and pencil
Coloured pencils

Draw a circle with a radius of 6cm. Inside it, draw a second circle radius 4.5cm and a third circle radius 3cm (see Fig A). Cut out and fold (with circle lines on the outside) into a half, a quarter, an eighth and sixteenth (see Fig B). Open back into an eighth and draw a petal shape using fold line for its centre (see Fig C). Cut out, open up and cut each petal down to the 3cm line (see Fig D). Flowers can now be decorated inside with coloured pencils. Fold over each petal towards centre, hiding decoration. Tuck in last petal (see Fig E). Float in a bowl of water and watch the lilies open up.

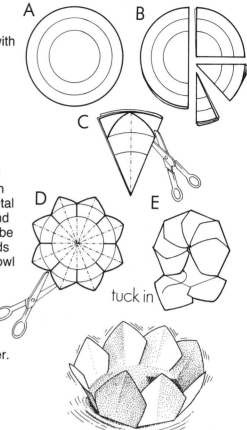

Frogs

As these are made entirely of plastic, they can be displayed in water.

Materials required

A roll of small plastic bags   Adhesive labels
Sand   Double sided adhesive tape
Elastic bands   White school glue
Green garden refuse bag

Fill each bag two-thirds full with sand. Secure tightly with an elastic band removing all air (see Fig F); children will probably need help to ensure that sand does not escape. Turn bag upside down, place on table and pat into the shape shown (Fig G). Using a ballpoint pen, mark arms, legs, head and spots on the green refuse bag and cut out. Use the guide in Fig H if required. Double sided adhesive tape is best for securing polythenes together (white glue is possible though it takes a long time to dry). Adhesive labels can be used to complete eyes and limbs.

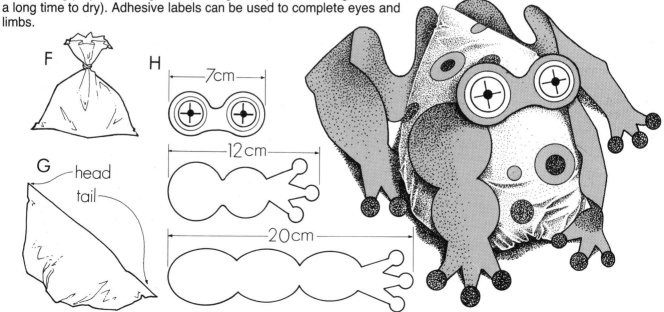

Spring display

An attractive spring display could be assembled if sufficient floor
space were available. Good daylight is necessary if the plants are to
thrive. A thick sheet of polythene would protect the flooring. Different
levels can be constructed out of orange boxes, breeze-blocks or
bricks, the display being as elaborate or as simple as space and
materials allow. Washing up bowls and ice cream containers lined with
pebbles could make small ponds in which to place the frogs and lilies
described on the previous page. Ideally the bowls would be sunk
below the bricks with the plastic edges softened by overhanging
plants. Further pot plants could provide a jungle like setting for the
cress and spider plant figures. Some children enjoy making miniature
gardens with moss twigs, cones and other found treasures. These
could be incorporated into the design with trays of germinated grass
seed and flowering bulbs. Seashore pebbles, sand and stones of
different sizes could provide extra textural interest.

Printed bouquet card

Materials required

Potatoes

Assorted coloured paints including green

Thick paper for card approx. 44cm × 60cm – folded in half

Gift wrapping ribbon

Petit four cutters – optional

Ruler

Thin kitchen sponge – optional

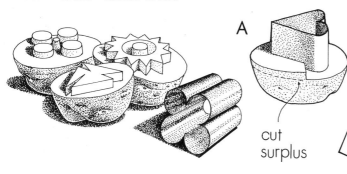

A

cut surplus

punch holes

Prepare potato cuts to provide a different floral design for each colour and a leaf design for the green paint. If the children are too young to cut the potatoes, metal petit four cutters can be used by teachers for ease. Push the cutter into the halved potato and cut surplus potato away (see Fig A). The shape can then be adapted to a leaf or flower. Mix up paint to a creamy consistency which can be painted directly on to the potato, or soak a thin kitchen sponge in paint and use as a print pad. First print green flower stems using the side of a ruler, crossing lines as in Fig B. Build up bouquet with flowers and leaves. Insert ribbon through two punched holes and tie into bow as in illustration.

B

30 cm

22 cm

'Feet up' card

Materials required

Thick paper for card approx. 50cm × 66cm (depending on the size of the feet)

Pink paint or pink paper

Fabric for collage or graph paper with coloured pens

White school glue

Fold thick white paper in half. If weather and nerves permit, each child stamps a pair of foot prints on the top half of their card. Failing this, draw round feet on pink paper (children can work in pairs) and cut out shapes, gluing on to the card. Younger children can draw or make a cushion collage. Older children could look at Victorian samplers and using pens on graph paper create a 'Victorian' footstool. All cards should bear the message 'Mum, put your feet up'.

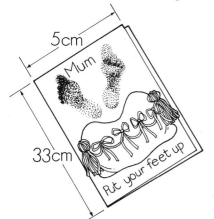

5 cm

Mum

33 cm

Put your feet up

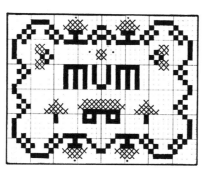

mum

Framed portrait card

Materials required

Thick brown paper approx.
42cm × 50cm

Corrugated cardboard

White paper approx.
10cm × 14cm

Pens and crayons

White school glue

Fold the thick paper into quarters to provide a stiff backing for collage (see Fig A). Each child draws a small portrait of their mother on the white paper. Glue this in the centre of the front of the card and decorate the surrounding frame with geometric shapes cut from the corrugated cardboard (see illustration).

Mum's mirror card

Materials required

Sheets of thick paper approx.
42cm × 50cm

Coloured paper

Mirror paper (sometimes sold for gift wrapping)

Sequins, doilies and pasta shapes for decoration

White school glue

Fold the thick paper in quarters as shown above. Children then create different types of mirrors using paper and collage materials. Ballpoints are best for marking mirror paper prior to cutting. Sticking can be a problem: white school glue, staples or double sided adhesive tape can all be used. Cards bear the message 'Who is the best Mum?'

Teapot card

Materials required

Thick white paper 20cm × 40cm

Tea bags on string

Pens and crayons

Adhesive tape

Fold the white paper in half. Children can draw round a tin for the basic circular shape of the teapot (see Fig B). The teacher then opens the card to cut a slit along the lid line.

Using pens and crayons, complete and decorate the teapot. A tea bag is then threaded through the card and held in place with adhesive tape (see Fig C). 'Make a cup of tea on Mothering Sunday' is the message.

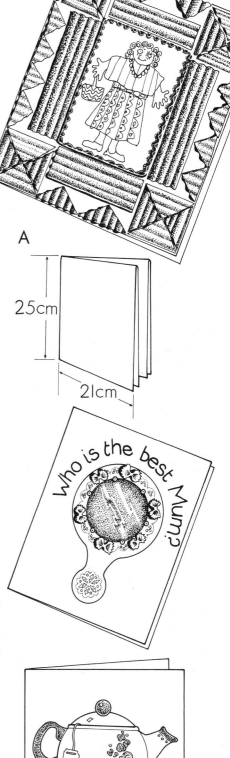

A

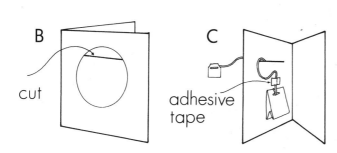

B

cut

C

adhesive tape

Simple square flower

Materials required

Thin paper   Coloured pens
Straws   Adhesive tape

Cut squares of paper approx. 10cm × 10cm. The children then
decorate their squares with coloured pens. Linear geometric shapes
look attractive (see illustration). Fold square into a half and then a
quarter hiding the decoration (see Fig A). Firm fold line with finger nail.
Unfold and refold across the diagonal into a half and then a quarter
(see Fig B). Firm fold line with finger nail. Unfold and push the sides of
the square towards the middle to form flower shape (see Fig C).
Secure flower to straw with adhesive tape (see Fig D).

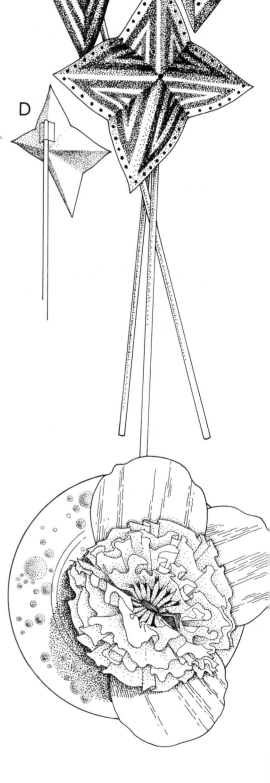

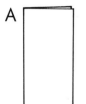 A   B 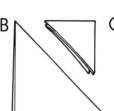   C 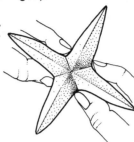   D

Water-lily

Displayed on a plate it can make an attractive gift for Mothering
Sunday.

Materials required

White or pastel crêpe paper   Large paper plate
Matching cotton thread   2 shades of very dilute blue paint
Light green crêpe paper for   White school glue
leaves

Prepare plate by dripping and splattering the blue paints over the
surface. Leave to dry. Cut four pieces of white or pastel crêpe paper
15cm × 25cm with the grain as in Fig E. Place on top of each other
and, with the 15cm end towards you, fold into a concertina. Bind
tightly round the middle with cotton and tie securely (see Fig F).
Separate and pull up each layer carefully towards the centre
stretching gently with thumbs (see Fig G). Cut three circles diameter
approx. 12cm from the green crêpe. Arrange and glue on to plate,
placing the lily on top.

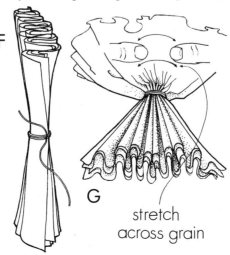

E

15cm | grain

|← 25 cm →|

F

G

stretch
across grain

Tissue flower

A very quick and simple flower to make.

Materials required

Tissue paper

Green house plant stakes approx. 30cm

Fluorescent pink paint – optional

Green crêpe paper – optional

For each flower cut six circles of tissue, diameter 20cm. Place on top of each other and make a crossed snip in the centre by folding centre of circles over (see Fig A). Push stick down the centre of circles and secure firmly with adhesive tape (Fig B). The tip of the stick can be dipped into pink paint. Carefully separate tissue layers. A more finished flower could have a bound stem. Cut a 2cm strip from a roll of green crêpe paper. Securing with white school glue, wrap crêpe strip round base of flower by twisting the stick, then gently pulling the strip diagonally away from the stem, twist the stick to cover the stem (see Fig C). Secure with glue.

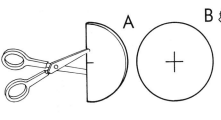

Crêpe daisy

Materials required

White crêpe paper

Contrast crêpe paper for centre of flower

Green crêpe paper

Cotton wool

Green house plant stake approx. 30cm

White school glue

Make a cotton wool ball. Cut a 10cm circle from the contrast crêpe paper and spread glue thinly round the edge. Place the circle glue-side down securing cotton wool on to top of stick (see Fig D). Cut two strips of white crêpe 14cm × 25cm and fold down centre of both (see Fig E). Glue cut edges of the two folded strips together applying glue sparingly. Fringe to within 1cm of cut edge (see Fig F). Wrap fringed strips around base of flower centre using minimum of glue. Bind stem as shown for tissue flower. Leaves can be added.

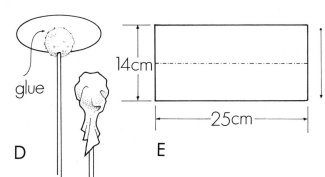

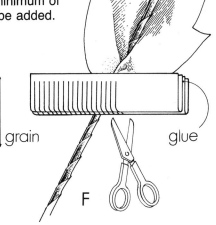

Paper sculpture flower

Very simple to make. It looks attractive in plain white paper but the children can decorate the flower before construction.

Materials required

Thin paper
Straws or house plant stakes
White school glue

Adhesive labels/coloured pens – optional

For each flower cut two squares of thin paper 10cm × 10cm. Fold each square across the diagonal and cut as Fig A. Unfold and glue the two cut corners of the squares together as in Fig B. Sandwiching the straw or stake, glue the two squares back to back so that the points form opposing diagonals (see Fig C).

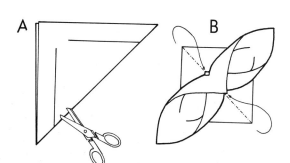
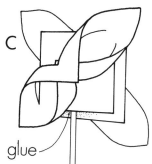

Cone-petalled flower

As with all these flowers, the glue needs to be applied sparingly; it is sometimes easier for children to apply it with cocktail sticks. These particular flowers look attractive on wall displays.

Materials required

Thin paper
Thicker paper of contrasting colour
Green house plant stakes approx. 30cm

White school glue
Adhesive tape
Paper clips – optional

Cut three circles of thin paper, diameter 10cm, and one circle of contrasting paper, diameter 10cm. Fold each circle in half and cut. Make semi-circles into cones and glue (see Fig D). When dry, using one of the thicker contrast cones as the centre, glue the six other cones round it. Paper clips can be used to hold the cones in position while the glue dries (see Fig E). Remove clips and secure to stake with adhesive tape (see Fig F.).

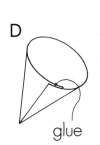
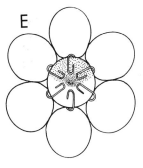
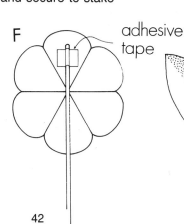

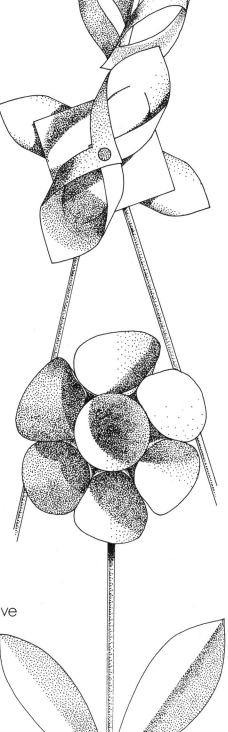

Triple-layered flower

Materials required

Thin paper of 2 contrasting colours

House plant sticks/straws

Corrugated card/sticky pads

White school glue

Adhesive tape

For each flower cut two circles, diameter 16cm and diameter 9cm, from one paper; and one circle, diameter 12cm, from the contrasting paper. Fold each circle into a half, a quarter and an eighth (see Fig A). Placing a round object of the same width as each circle segment draw lightly round it and cut (see Fig B). Unfold and assemble flower with largest petalled shape at back. For a three-dimensional effect glue a small piece of corrugated card or sticky pad between each layer. Complete flower with a plain circle of contrast paper for centre. Secure to stake/straw with adhesive tape.

A

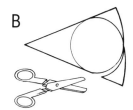
B

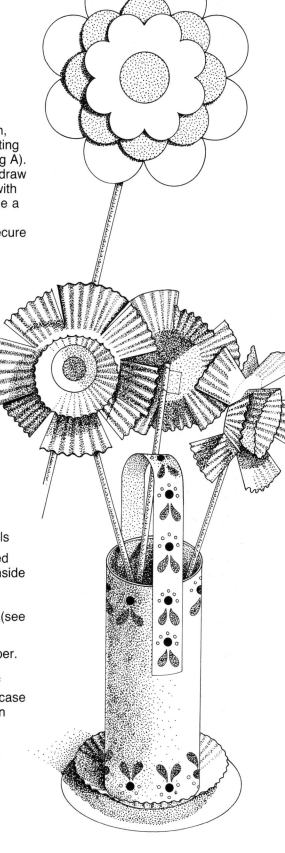

Daffodil baskets

Simple enough for very young children. The filled baskets can make a gift to take home for Mothering Sunday or Easter.

Materials required

White paper cake cases

Sweet/petit four paper cases – white if possible

Straws

Toilet roll tube

Paper

White school glue

Coloured pens/adhesive labels

Flatten a paper cake case and make eight cuts into the corrugated sides. Every other segment can be folded back (see Fig C). The inside of the sweet paper case (if not available, use a cake paper case) can be decorated with faces or adhesive labels coloured yellow and orange to resemble daffodils. Glue on to prepared cake case (see Fig D) and secure to straw with adhesive tape.

To make basket – cover toilet roll tube with white or coloured paper. Trim ends. Cut a handle from a strip of paper 1.5cm × 20cm. Decorate handle and tube before gluing handle well down side of tube. Cut a circle of paper diameter 10cm. Glue a flattened cake case on to the circle. Dip bottom of toilet roll tube into glue and stick on to flattened cake case. Place daffodils inside.

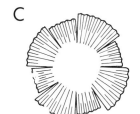
C

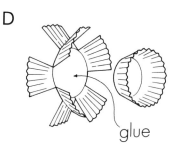
D

glue

Paper ball chicks

An adult will have to help younger children as staples are required to fix parts together.

Materials required

Yellow tissue/crêpe paper

Card

Bendable straws

Pink/orange paper

Large adhesive labels

Stapler

White school glue

Cotton for suspending chicks

Cut a small square of card 4cm × 4cm. Take two bendable straws and carefully fringe the bottom. Splay the spikes out to form the feet of the chick. Staple legs on to the square of card (see Fig A). Cut eight circles of tissue/crêpe paper, diameter 16cm. Fold each circle into a quarter and arrange four of them on one side of the card as in Fig B. Tack down with a little glue and then staple in place. Turn card over and secure the other four circles in a similar manner. Carefully open up each circle until a good ball shape is achieved. Cut a square from the pink/orange paper 5cm × 5cm. Fold across the diagonal and place adhesive label eyes on the fold as in Fig C. This can then be attached to the chick ball as in illustration. Bend the legs as required and suspend with cotton.

A

B

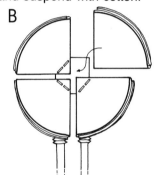

C

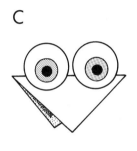

Easter nests

Materials required

Cardboard apple tray available from greengrocers

As many different types of brown paper as the children can find

Small feathers

White school glue

Small dried flowers – optional

Cut up apple tray into individual nest shapes. Cut brown papers into small strips approx. 5cm × 0.5cm. More variety is achieved by cutting some with pinking shears. Cover the underside of nest by gluing paper strips criss-cross over surface. When dry, turn nest over and repeat, finishing with feathers and perhaps a few dried flowers. Sugar eggs might mysteriously appear on the last day of term.

Easter rabbits

Papier mâché applied over balloons can be very time consuming. This project has the slight advantage of producing two rabbits from each balloon, allowing children to work in pairs, thus speeding up the process.

Materials required for a pair of Rabbits

Pear shaped balloon	Brown wrapping paper
Vaseline	Tissue paper
Newspaper/pink newsprint/yellow pages	Paper, adhesive labels, cotton wool for decorating
Wall paper paste suitable for children	Plastic flower pot or other container to hold balloon steady

Blow up balloon, knotting securely, and cover with Vaseline for preservation. Tear up newspaper into pieces roughly 3cm × 5cm. Place base of balloon into flower pot to keep upright. Applying paste to torn newspaper, cover top of balloon with overlapping pieces. Turn balloon over and cover bottom. Let each layer dry before starting the next (if left in the flower pot turn over to dry, otherwise the bottom will remain soggy). Alternate layers with contrast coloured newsprint to show up any gaps. The balloon will probably need three such layers before applying a final layer of brown wrapping paper torn into small pieces. The rabbits in the photograph were completed with patches of white and grey tissue pasted on top. When papier mâché is dry, an adult can cut the shape in half with a pair of large sharp scissors. Ears, nose, whiskers and teeth can be cut out of paper (ears perhaps lined with pink crêpe). Adhesive labels may be used for eyes and cotton wool for the tail.

On Page 49, two of the rabbits were worn as Easter Bonnets. Hat elastic was stapled to the sides of the rabbit.

Hatching chicks card

Materials required

Paper for eggs – effective if
splattered first with paint

Paper for background

Orange paper

Glue

Circular sponge

Yellow paint

Coloured pens

Draw and cut out whole and broken egg shapes (a template of a
complete egg might be helpful). Glue on to card. Paint the underside
of the sponge yellow, and print chicks hatching out of eggs. Leave to
dry. Cut out diamond shape from orange paper. Fold in half and glue
on chicks creating three-dimensional beaks. Complete with coloured
pens.

Spring hare card

This is suitable for older children as drawing and cutting skills are
required (unless a template is used). The method of using a coiled
pipe cleaner to create both a three-dimensional effect and movement
can be useful in any card or wall display.

Materials required

Assortment of thick papers

Pipe cleaners

Glue

Adhesive tape

Adhesive labels – optional

Coloured crayons/pens

Fold a piece of paper approx. 40cm × 30cm into a half and then a
quarter to provide a stiff backing (see Fig A). Open as in illustration
and draw grassy background. Draw and cut jumping hare using
assorted papers, pens and adhesive labels. Whiskers can be made
from very narrow strips of white paper. Coil pipe cleaner round a tube
or handle about 2cm diameter. Attach one end of coil to the back of
the hare with adhesive tape and the other end firmly to the card so
that hare is hidden when card is closed (see Fig A).

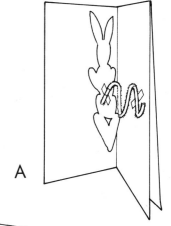

A

Printed woolly sheep card

Materials required

White, black and assorted green papers
Tissue paper
Pipe cleaners
Black or grey paint
Glue
Pencils or crayons

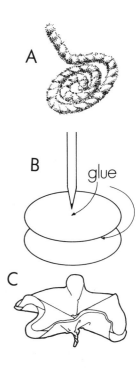

Draw the rough shape of a sheep's body on white paper. Coil the pipe cleaner round leaving the end upright (see Fig A). Holding the end, paint the underside of the coil and print the wool coat. Cut out and glue on to background. Complete the sheep as wished. The flowers in the photograph were made from two circles of tissue paper. Put a spot of glue between them and in the centre of the top circle. Push a pencil or a pointed object into the centre (see Fig B), and twist tissue round point to make flower (see Fig C).

This card can be adapted for Christmas, in which case grey or white paint could be printed onto black paper and completed with stars and shepherd.

Chick with opening beak card

Materials required

Paper for card
Crayons/pens/yellow blackboard chalk
Adhesive labels

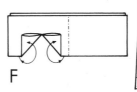

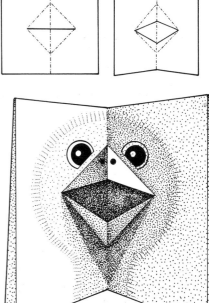

Cut a piece of paper approx. 30cm × 18cm. Fold into a half and then a quarter (see Fig D). Refold along the length and make a cut 5cm long, 7cm from the end (see Fig E). This may be roughly judged by younger children. Fold triangles of paper both towards and away from you (see Fig F), firming fold line with finger nail. Open card and refold across centre with beak towards you (see Fig G). Carefully close card up allowing beak to open (see Fig H). Flatten card and draw around a circular object for chick's head. Colour beak orange and plumage yellow. The outline can be softened with yellow blackboard chalk smudged by finger. The inside of the beak may be coloured too. Complete card by drawing or using adhesive labels for eyes and nostrils.

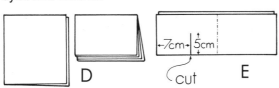

Easter chain

Seasonal chains can look very decorative when suspended in school halls or corridors. It is an opportunity for classes to co-operate, each class choosing a particular object in the chain for all of their children to make. This way long chains of decorations can be made relatively quickly. The effect is enhanced if certain colours or papers are common to each object which visually will link the work from different classes. For example in the photograph the chickens could be made by one class, the sheep by a second and the flowers by a third. Each include the colours pink, white and yellow. Paper clips or Blu-Tack, can be used to prevent decorations from sliding together.

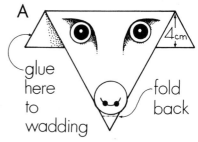

A

Materials required for Sheep

White terylene wadding (sold by the yard for quilting)	White and pink paper
	White school glue
Paper doilies	Pens
White straws	Adhesive labels – optional

Stick two straws directly on to doily to represent legs. Cut circle of wadding diameter 18cm and glue on top of doily. Draw an equilateral triangle sides 18cm (a template might be useful). Turn 4cm of one side under (see Fig A). Draw face using pink circle for nose and include yellow in the eyes. Adhesive labels may be used. Glue along back strip and attach to wadding. Fold back point below nose (see Fig A).

B

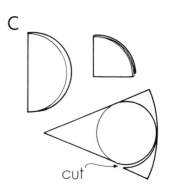

Materials required for Flowers

Green tissue paper	Glue
White, pink and yellow paper	Pens
White paper cake cases	

Cut a 20cm square of green tissue paper. Fold into a half, a quarter and an eighth. Holding by the centre, cut into leaf shape (see Fig B). Cut a circle of white paper diameter 15cm, fold into a half, a quarter and an eighth. Having placed a round object of the same width as the segment, lightly draw round it and cut out as in Fig C. Glue white flower shape on to tissue leaf, gluing cake case on top decorated with pink and yellow paper. The flowers in the photograph were completed with insect drawings.

See Page 44 for instructions to make chicken.

C

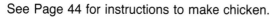

Easter bonnets

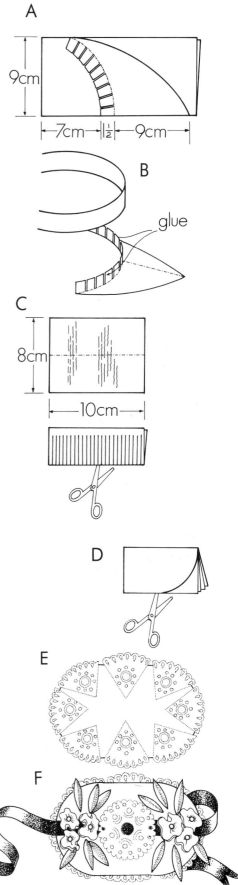

Materials required for Beaked Cap

Thin card for template	Adhesive labels
Yellow paper for head band	Pens
Orange paper for beak	White school glue
Yellow crêpe paper	Staples

Cut yellow head bands approx. 4cm × 64cm. Prepare a template for beak from a piece of card 18cm × 18cm. Fold card in half and draw shape following dimensions given in Fig A. Cut and unfold. Using template draw beak on to orange paper. Cut out. Fold cut section upright applying glue to the front (see Fig B) and glue to the inside centre of head band. Whilst band is drying, cut piece of yellow crêpe 8cm × 10cm (see Fig C). Fold in half and fringe. Mark position of eyes on head band. Coil crêpe fringe round the mark and attach as in photograph. Complete eyes and nostrils with decorated labels. Staple head band to required length.

Materials required for Flowered Bonnets

Coloured papers including green	Adhesive labels
Paper doilies	Paper ribbon from florists or strips
Tissue paper	of crêpe width 6cm
	White school glue

Take a piece of coloured paper approx. 30cm × 40cm. Fold into a half and then a quarter. Round off the corners (as in Fig D) to make an oval shape when unfolded. Line underneath with projecting pieces of doily (see Fig E). Turn over and glue 1.5 metres of ribbon or crêpe strip along width of hat. Decorate with doilies, tissue flowers (see Page 47), adhesive labels and green leaves folded lengthwise in half, to give three-dimensional effect (see Fig F).

See Page 45 for instructions to make rabbit.

Chrysalis and butterfly

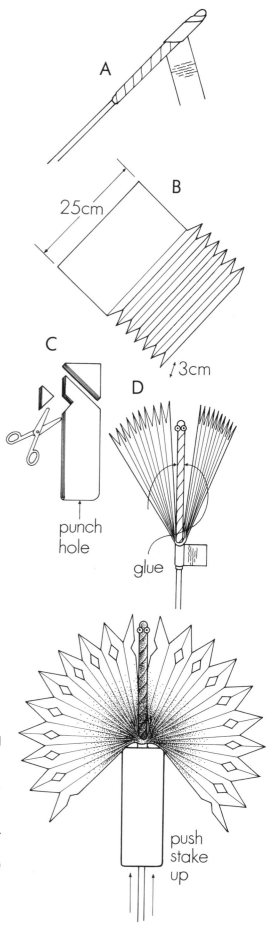

Suitable for older children as folding skills are needed.

Materials required

Bright coloured tissue paper	Dark paper
Bright coloured crêpe paper	White school glue
Small house plant stakes	Small adhesive labels
Toilet roll tube	Pens or paint

Make a mark 10cm from the top of the plant stake. Cut across roll of crêpe paper to make strips 1.5 cm wide. Putting a small dab of glue on the 10cm mark, wind the crêpe round the stake. Twist the stake, covering to the top and back down again to form butterfly body (see Fig A). Eyes may be added.

Cut rectangles of tissue paper 25cm × 70cm (a normal sheet cut in half lengthways). Fold into pleats 3cm wide (see Fig B). Fold pleated paper in half and cut as in Fig C. Make hole in centre bottom of folded pleats. Push bottom of garden stake down through hole until butterfly body reaches pleats (see Fig D). Put a small dab of glue on stake under pleats and wind crêpe strip round stake to keep tissue in place. Apply a little glue down both sides of the body so that the first pleat sticks to it.

Cover toilet roll tube with dark paper and decorate with labels, paint or pens. Put the bottom of the stake through the tube and carefully pull the tube up to cover the butterfly. Holding the tube, push the stake up to allow the butterfly to emerge with its wings open (see illustration).

N.B. Hold butterfly downwards before re-covering with tube.

Pecking birds

Tap the blue tit's tail to help him get the milk.

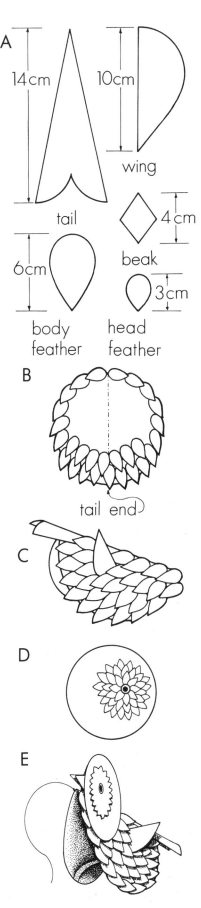

Materials required

Card for templates – optional
Large paper plates
Assorted yellow papers including tissue and crêpe
White tissue

Blue paper
White school glue
Adhesive labels – optional
Masking tape
Blu-Tack

The plates need to be prepared by an adult scoring a line down the centre of the back. If templates are to be used these too should be prepared (see Fig A). Using many different yellow papers, the children draw and cut out body feathers. Apply glue sparingly to the plate and place the feathers in layers, pointed end towards the tail end of plate (see Fig B). Draw and cut a tail and two wings from the blue paper. Fold plate in half and fold tail along the length. Glue tail and wings, tucking them into feathers as in Fig C. Draw and cut two circles diameter 12cm from the blue paper. Draw and cut face feathers from white tissue. Applying glue sparingly to area round eye on both circles, glue white feathers in circular layers (see Fig D). Eyes can be completed with an adhesive label. Cut a diamond shape from yellow paper and fold in half to form beak. Spread glue on the back of both head circles. Glue one on one side of body as in photograph and place the other on the other side to match, sandwiching the beak between the two circles. Complete the bird by attaching a bridge of masking tape across the bottom and place a piece of Blu-Tack under head to aid pecking motion (see Fig E).

Pecking birds could make a winter display, in which case robins pecking at bread crumbs would remind children to feed the birds during cold weather.

These are our sunbeam plates.

We chose hot summer colours.

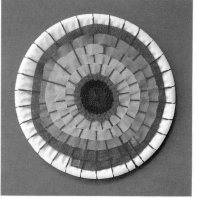

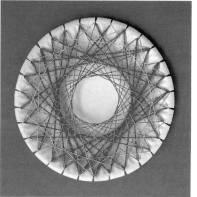

Sunbeam plates

The designs photographed were produced by seven year olds. Patience is required for the woven plates and counting skills required for the filigree plates; however, even if the designs are accomplished without accuracy they still look attractive.

Materials required

Large paper plates

Threads of every thickness and texture eg. sewing cotton, knitting cotton, wool, string, lurex, metallic thread, raffia, ribbon

Strips of crêpe paper

Thick blunt wool needles

Adhesive tape

Depending on the ability of the children, the plates might well have to be prepared in advance, which can be time consuming. Older children should be able to mark out and cut the plates themselves. The plates we bought had an embossed pattern near the edge which was used as a guide to mark and cut 30 slots (see Fig A). In order to make the 'spokes' for the woven plates, tape a thickish thread to the back of the plates and pull through a slot to the front (see Fig B). Pull thread across the centre front of the plate, down the opposite slot and up through the next one (see Fig C). Continue to cross over front of plate to opposite slot until the spokes are complete (see Fig D and Fig E). Turn plate over and tape down end of thread (see Fig F). The plate is now prepared for weaving.

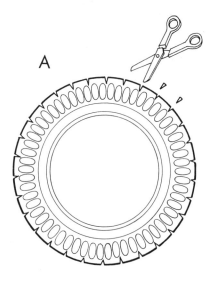

A

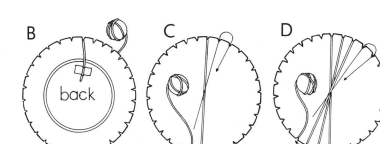

The segmented sun design

A length of thread is cut and taped to the back of the 'spoked' plate. Pull thread through one of the slots to the front and thread through needle (see Fig G). Weave in and out of the chosen number of spokes (see Fig H). Continue weaving towards centre. Bind thread round and hide the end by threading back through work. Segments can be of varying widths and textures; some can be sub-divided at the top to add interest (see Fig I). Experiment with ideas. Beads and scraps may be woven into the design.

The circular sun design

In order to produce the circular woven effect it is necessary to have an uneven number of spokes. Use a plate prepared with 30 'spokes' as above. Cut a length of thread and tape it to the back of the plate. Cut an extra slot between two others and pull the thread through it to the front (see Fig J). This thread becomes the extra uneven spoke. Thread it through a needle and pull over the centre. Start to weave it in and out of the spokes (see Fig K). This is difficult at first but once a few rows have been achieved it becomes easier. Build up circles in different colours and textures. Strips of crêpe paper are rewarding in that the circle grows quickly, but care needs to be taken to prevent the strips from twisting.

The filigree sun design

Use a plate prepared with 30 slots. See instructions and Fig A on previous page. Thread is taped to the back of the plate and pulled through a slot to the front as in Fig B. Then working in the same direction round the plate, the child chooses a number (eg. 10 as in Fig L) and counts it out, pulling the thread into the appropriate slot and bringing it up through the next one. Omitting the slot that the wool is pulled through, start counting again from the slot ahead. Continue the same number until the thread doubles over itself and the pattern is complete. Pull the thread through to the back and fasten with tape. Figures L–N show the emerging pattern that number ten would make on a plate prepared with 30 slots. The higher the number, the more the threads cover the plate; conversely a low number will produce a design which remains close to the rim. When using 30 slots, the highest workable number is 13, and the lowest suggested number is 7.

Prior to starting, the children wrote the colour of their thread beside the chosen number for reference. In some cases they completed their designs with 3 different threads and numbers worked over each other. The most enthusiastic embarked on the small plates in the photograph which, having 42 slots, allowed numbers as high as 18 to be counted out.

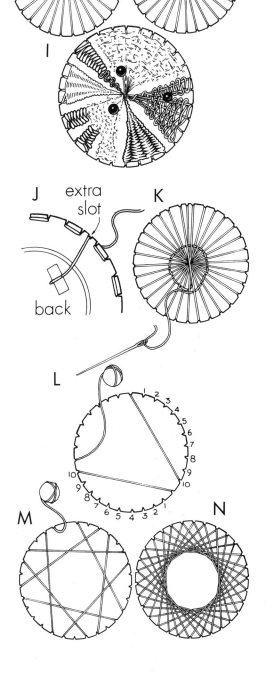

Rocking yachts

Materials required

Large paper plates

Blue, turquoise and green felt-tip
and ball point pens

Blue, turquoise and green tissue
paper

White paper

White school glue

Masking tape – optional

Blu-Tack/Plasticine – optional

An adult will need to prepare the plates. Placing laminate side up, find
the centre of the plate and score two parallel lines 4cm apart with a
sharp knife against a metal ruler (see Fig A). The children then draw a
seascape on to plate using felt-tips and ball point pens. Bend plate as
in Fig B and complete decoration with wavy strips of tissue paper
glued on to the edge of the plate.

The yacht requires a 15cm square piece of paper. Fold across both
diagonals as in Fig C, and cut along one diagonal fold to the centre
of square. Fold in half along other diagonal (see Fig D). Fold bottom
corner up (see Fig E). Fold lower point of boat back (see Fig F). Once
yacht is decorated it can be glued on to centre of plate. The two sides
of the plate are then held in place by a bridging piece of masking tape
or paper (see Fig G). Flags, sailors, fishing lines are all possible
additions. A piece of Blu-Tack or Plasticine placed as illustrated will
aid rocking motion and sea sickness.

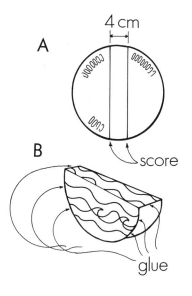

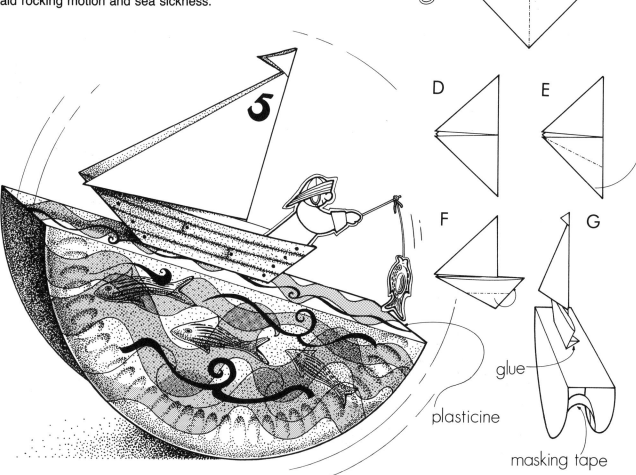

Sports day – running sportsman

It is a possible activity for the customary wet sportsday. Suitable for older children as drawing skills are necessary.

Materials required

Thin white card
Pencils/crayons
Paper fasteners

Prepare pieces of card 15cm × 10cm. Filling the card from top to bottom, the children draw a running figure to include shorts but no legs (see Fig A). Cut round figure and punch hole 1cm above centre of bottom edge.

Cut a circle of card diameter 10cm. Using a pencil, lightly divide the circle into four quarters (see Fig B). Using the pencil line as a guide for positioning, draw four identical legs and feet facing the same direction (see Fig C). Punch hole in centre of circle.

Placing the body over the legs, fix the two pieces of card together with a paper fastener. 'Run' along surface.

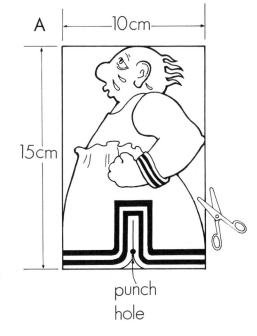

A | ←—10cm—→

15cm

punch
hole

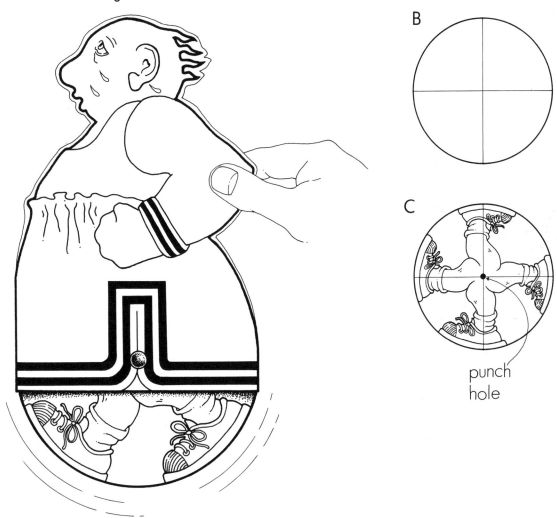

B

C

punch
hole

THE SCHOOL FAIR

The annual Fair is an important social event and an invaluable means of raising money for a school. Though not part of the classroom curriculum it is worth mentioning as it is often the task of teachers as well as parents to put forward fresh ideas each year. Schools fortunate enough to have an active Parent – Teachers association have fewer problems providing a body of people to organize the work. Perhaps labour is more willing if parents are given materials and specific tasks to do; this of course requires organisation. It is worth bearing in mind that anything made especially for a fair should be relatively simple and quick to produce. Many parents are disheartened, having worked for days on handmade objects, to see them sold for a few pence, which barely covers the cost of the materials used. This makes no financial sense. If beautiful handmade articles are contributed, it is much better that they are reserved for prizes.

Perhaps the most helpful starting point is to choose a theme. This can spark off ideas for objects to sell, games to play, fancy dress and indeed decorations for stalls. Teddy bears proved a successful theme in our local school. Clowns, circuses, snowmen, pirates, haunted houses, monsters, extra terrestrial, jungles, robots, a period in history or even a particular colour could all stimulate the imagination.

I have chosen the theme of Summer and in the next few pages have tried to show how it could be incorporated into activities.
I have anticipated that adults carry out much of the work, but in some cases the children themselves would help.

A sun design is the main visual link and this could be used in making paper badges, earrings, hats and decorations. All could be made quite quickly and sold. Use a good quality bright yellow paper ensuring the articles are attractive. Templates in strong card need to be made so that a parent can trace round and cut a large number of suns from one sheet of paper using either scissors or a sharp knife against a metal ruler. The design for the badge and earrings have been drawn the correct size so they can be traced for the initial template.

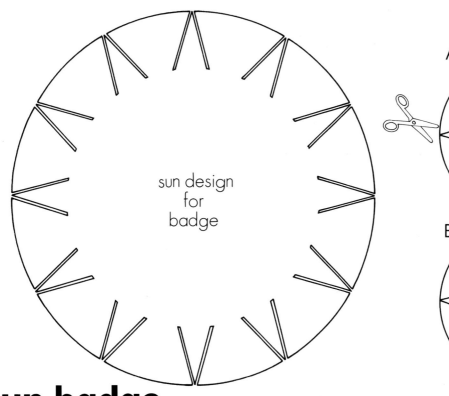

sun design
for
badge

A

B

C

Sun badge

Materials required

Heavy card

Good quality yellow paper

Labels

Pens

Double sided adhesive tape

Trace sun design on to heavy card and cut out with sharp knife and metal ruler. Draw round template on to paper and cut out design (see Fig A). Fold the shape between the points towards the centre, overlapping evenly (see Fig B). Complete sun design with face made from adhesive labels and pens (see Fig C). Place a piece of double sided adhesive tape on the back leaving top protective layer for wearer to remove.

Sun earrings

Materials and method are the same as above except that the initial template is smaller. The earrings are of course sold in pairs. Double sided adhesive tape adheres to skin quite satisfactorily.

sun design
for
earrings

Sun hats

1 Sun badge (see above)

White paper

Turquoise blue pen

Staples

Take a strip of paper approx. 60cm long. Using blue pen, draw a cloud design along length. Cut out, leaving small white border outside pen line (see Fig D). Glue sun on to front of hat and staple back to fit individual heads (see Fig E).

D

E

Spot-the-sun game

Materials required

Thick sheet of polystyrene as large as possible

Masking tape – optional

Paper – white/grey/black

Pens

Rubber-based glue
(eg. Copydex)

Pins

Adhesive labels

Prize

If wished, the polystyrene sheet can be protected by masking tape carefully applied over edge, mitring the corners (see Fig A). A thick black line drawn with felt marker inside the tape will improve the appearance. A small sun is then drawn directly on to the sheet with a felt-tip pen. Using papers, several children paint or draw clouds of different sizes which are cut out and glued on to the polystyrene with rubber-based glue. The clouds should cover the sun and most of the surface, but do not apply the glue directly onto the sun.

Contestants pay an entry fee, write their name and telephone number on an adhesive label which is bent round a pin and stuck where the sun is thought to be hiding.

At the end of the day the person who knows where the sun is drawn carefully peels off clouds and decides who is nearest the target. Prize for winner.

A

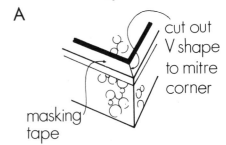

cut out V shape to mitre corner

masking tape

Have-a-sunprize game

Materials required

Blue paper

Paints

Pens

Rubber-based glue
(eg. Copydex)

Bright adhesive labels

Small prizes

Cover large wall area with blue paper which could be decorated with clouds. As many children as possible paint or draw small suns which are cut out and collected together. One in five suns have bright adhesive labels glued firmly on to the back. All suns are then glued on to blue backing, applying rubber-based glue sparingly.

Contestants pay an entry fee which allows them to peel off a sun. Those finding bright labels on the back win a small prize. If suns are decorative enough they could be worn afterwards.

Ball-in-the-mouth game

Definitely for adults to construct, but children could help to decorate faces.

Materials required

Thick corrugated cardboard cut from grocery boxes

Thin fabric, preferably red or pink

Staples

String

Coloured papers, felt, fabrics, paint, pens and scraps

White school glue

Old tennis balls

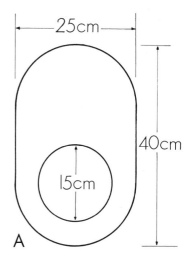

A

Draw oval shape approx. 40cm × 25cm on corrugated cardboard. Cut shape out with sharp knife (don't try to cut through thickness in one stroke – cut through gradually). Cut circle for mouth diameter 15cm (see Fig A). Turn card to back and mark out twelve points round mouth (see Fig B). Cut a 30cm diameter circle from fabric and mark it in a similar way. Matching marks, staple fabric to card through mouth (see Fig C). Make two holes with skewer so that head can be suspended by string (see Fig D). Draw and decorate heads using paper, scraps etc.

B   fabric

Hang a little distance from a wall or net so that balls are contained. Depending on what anchorage is available for lines, it might be more eye catching to suspend two rows of heads. Experiment to find suitable distance to throw tennis balls.

According to how the shapes are decorated, this game would lend itself to many different themes.

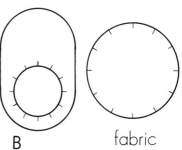

C

D

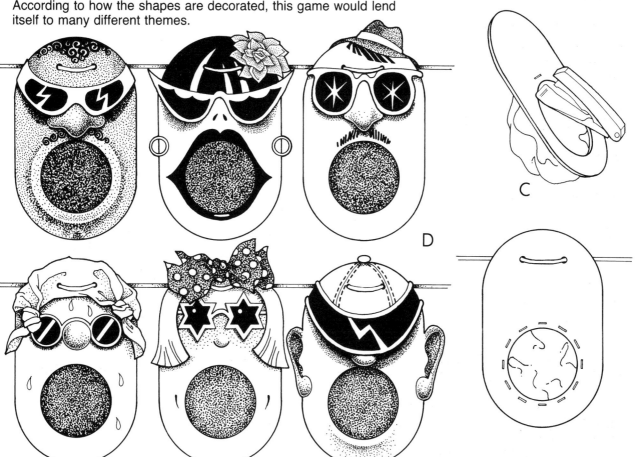

Decorating the stall – balloon and baskets

Children can help make these decorations which are then sold at the fair.

Materials required for each Balloon

A round balloon	Large adhesive labels
A paper cup	Adhesive tape
Coloured paper	Coloured pens
Crêpe paper	White school glue

Make the basket first. Cut a strip of crêpe paper width approx. 4cm with the grain running the length (see Fig A). Apply a dab of glue at regular intervals and twist the strip of crêpe as shown in Fig B. Glue twisted crêpe round cup to form bunting. Use coloured pens to complete decoration (see Fig C).

Preferably with the use of a guillotine, or an adult with a sharp knife, cut several strips of coloured paper 1cm width and approx. 40cm long. Blow up balloons and knot securely. The larger the balloon, the longer the strips of paper will need to be. If wished, these strips can be decorated by the children; they are then positioned decorative side down on to a large sticky-side-up label, as in Fig D. Turn label sticky side down and fix on top of balloon (see Fig E). A further four strips can be stuck on to a second label and applied over the first (see Fig F). Glue or tape ends of strips inside decorated cup at correct spacing (see illustration).

Figures could be cut to place inside baskets. The balloons could be attached to the wall with double sided adhesive tape or, better still, suspended by cotton attached with adhesive tape on top of label.

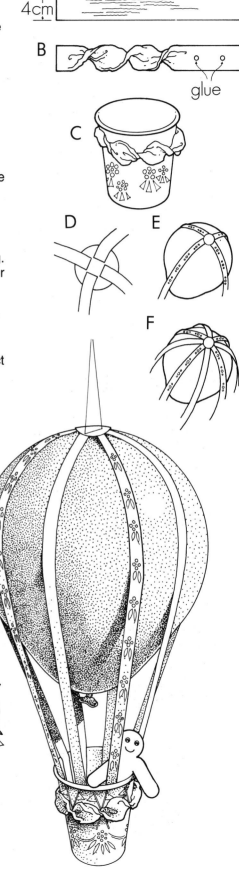

Decorative baking

Home baking always sells quickly and the refreshment stall could easily reflect the summer theme. Small cakes and biscuits can be decorated with suns or appropriate designs. Ready-made fondant icing, rolled out and cut into shapes, is a simple way of applying a motif to small cakes.

Attractive coloured glazes can be made by beating an egg yolk with a drop of water and adding different food colourings; these are then painted directly on to biscuits before baking.

It is worth looking in confectionery shops for sweets which can add a decorative topping when arranged on glace icing.

Why not run a decorate-a-cake competition? Both children and parents could decorate a cake they had made based on the theme of the fair. A raffle could be run alongside the table where the cakes are exhibited. The winning ticket would receive the cake judged to be best and the rest of the cakes could be auctioned individually to the highest bidders.

The need for masks can arise at any time throughout the school year. Plays and special assemblies often require the transformation of children into unlikely creatures. However, masks can present problems; if they cover the entire face, the child seldom has adequate vision. Masks can prove hot, uncomfortable and sometimes frightening for the wearer; they can also be difficult to secure.

On the following pages there are some suggestions for masks, all based on the same method of construction but each adapted to a different bird or animal. They have proved practical to make and wear. The basic mask is cut out of a flat piece of paper, part of which is cut into strips fitting over the back of the head.
The mask is then secured on to a paper head band fitted to the child's head. It is at such an angle that if the child holds his head up he sees under the mask; if he looks down the mask is completely visible to onlookers. At no time does the child look through the mask.

Goose, swan and duck masks

Materials required

Thin card for template
Paper of required colours
Crêpe paper of required colours
Adhesive labels of varying sizes
– optional

White school glue
Staples

An adult will need to make templates out of thin card. Using a ruler and a compass, draw mask template from dimensions given in Fig A. Trace beak to make separate template. Cut out both templates leaving a slot between strips at top of mask to allow children to mark width of strips. Cut out eyes. The children draw around templates on to paper. The mask and beak are then cut out leaving eyes marked but *not* cut. Glue beak on to mask. An adult will need to score down centre of mask, fold in half and open again.

Cut strips of crêpe approx. 25cm × 5cm across grain (see Fig B). Fold down centre and fringe along cut edges (see Fig C). Apply glue on a 9cm circle round both eye marks. Glue fringed strip in circle (see Fig D). Glue second strip inside first circle round eye mark. Complete with decorated adhesive labels (see Fig E).

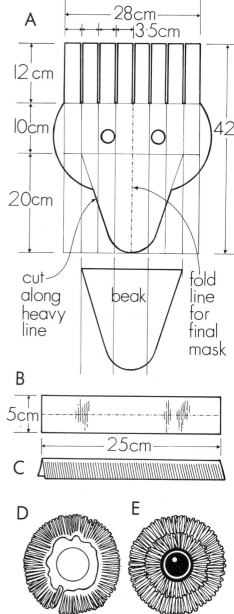

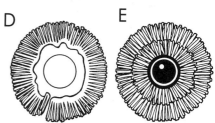

Gather strips together (as in Fig F) to shape mask. Secure with staples – always use stapler so that long smooth side of staple has contact with head and hair. Cut head band width 4cm to fit each individual head and secure mask on to it at correct angle (see Fig G).

The basic bird mask can be adapted. Swans need the distinctive beak markings and are improved with smaller eyes. We gave the mallard ducks blue and green crêpe fringes encircling each eye, and rounded off the end of the beak.

If available, feathers would provide an excellent alternative for decoration.

Mouse mask

Materials required

Thin card for template	Pink and white crayons
Paper of required colour	Thick white, grey and brown paint
White paper	Black felt-tip pens
Staples	

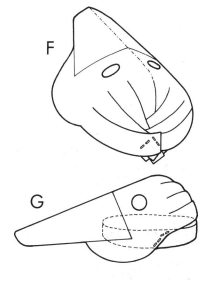

Follow instructions on previous page concerning mask template using measurements given in Fig H. Children draw round template and cut out mask leaving eyes and nose marked but *not* cut. An adult will need to score down three centre fold lines shown in Fig H. Fold mask and open again

We completed the mouse features by crayoning the ears and nose pink. A white crayon was used round the eyes and nose. The eyes were filled in with black felt-tip pen with a highlight of a small white circle. Rather than saturate the paper with wet paint, we printed fur by dipping small lengths of balsa wood into thick paint. Strips of heavy card would do as well. We concentrated on the areas round the ears, eyes and nose.

Whiskers can be made from long narrow strips of white paper threaded through holes punched round the nose area (see photograph).

Assemble mouse mask as with bird mask, stapling on to head band. Bend ears up.

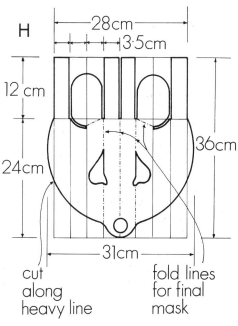

63

Horse mask

Materials required

Thin card for template
Paper of required colour
White/grey/brown tissue
Adhesive labels – optional
White school glue

White paint
Sponge
Black/brown felt-tip pens
Staples

Follow instructions on Page 62 concerning mask template using measurements given in Fig A on this page. Children draw round template and cut out mask leaving eyes and nostrils marked but *not* cut. An adult will need to score down fold lines on ears and face of mask shown in Fig A. Fold mask and open again. Shape ears as in photograph.

If the head is to be decorated, dip sponge into white paint and then squeeze out excess paint. Make light short 'brush strokes' on mask to create soft coat. Complete ears and nostrils with felt-tip pens, and eyes with pens and adhesive labels if wished.

Cut strips of assorted tissue paper approx 3cm × 50cm. Make mane by gluing strips on top of each other, criss-crossing as in Fig B. Strips may be fringed where they are to hang over face.

Having lifted up ears, assemble horse mask as with bird mask. Staple on to head band at correct angle and glue mane between ears.

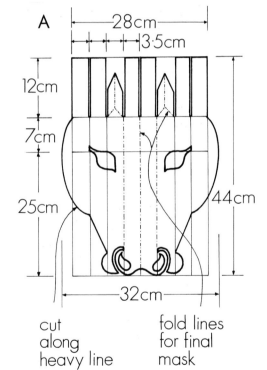

A

28cm
3·5cm
12cm
7cm
25cm
44cm
32cm

cut along heavy line

fold lines for final mask

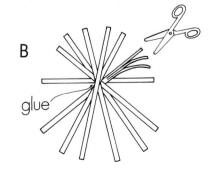

B

glue

Sheep mask

Materials required

Thin card for template
White/grey paper
White crêpe paper – optional
Adhesive labels – optional
Cotton wool

Black and brown felt-tip pens
Black and pink crayons
White school glue
Staples

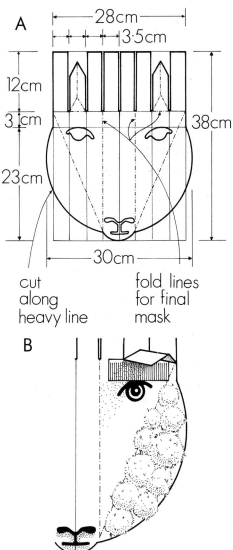

A

28cm
3·5cm
12cm
3·cm
23cm
38cm
30cm

cut
along
heavy line

fold lines
for final
mask

B

Follow instructions on Page 62 concerning mask template, using measurements given in Fig A on this page. Children draw round template and cut out mask leaving eyes and nostrils marked but *not* cut. An adult will need to score down fold lines on ears and face of mask shown in Fig A. Fold mask and open again.

Complete eyes with black and brown felt-tip pens using adhesive labels if wished. Colour front of ears pink, this becoming the underside when shaped along fold lines, as in photograph. Complete nose using the black felt-tip pen and black and pink crayons.

Make small balls of cotton wool by lightly rolling in hands, and glue on to areas either side of the face (see Fig B). If wished, eye lashes can be applied above the eyes. Cut a strip of crêpe paper approx. 9cm × 3cm and fringe. Glue along top of strip as in Fig B.

Having positioned ears, assemble sheep mask as with bird mask. Staple on to head band at correct angle.

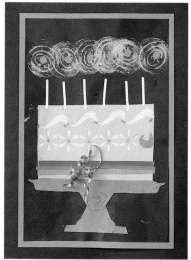

Birthday cake card

Printing candle light with a cut onion is simple and can be adapted to birthday occasions, school anniversaries or indeed Christmas cards and Christmas friezes.

Materials required

An onion	Yellow paint
Dark paper for background	Paint, pens and paper, ribbon for decoration
Mixed coloured papers for cake, plate, candles and flames	White school glue

Cut onion in half across the middle to reveal ring shapes. Leave for 24 hours to allow onion to shrink, producing a more textured print.

Assemble card by cutting candles, cake and plate out of coloured paper. Glue in position. Using a plastic fork, lift onion half and brush yellow paint on to cut surface. Print excess paint on to rough paper until rings show clearly, then print on top of candles. Complete card by adding candle flames and decorating cake with pens and ribbons. Cherries and cake decorations can be printed using pencil ends dipped in paint.

Birthday badges

Birthday badges are sometimes distributed during birthday assemblies. Plain card badges backed on to safety pins can be bought and then decorated with a child's name and age; however, if time can be found, an attractive badge could be made. The badges in the photograph are a simplified version of the sun badge shown on Page 57 and are quick to make.

Materials required for each badge

Bright coloured paper

Bright adhesive label

Double sided adhesive tape

Paper ribbon – optional

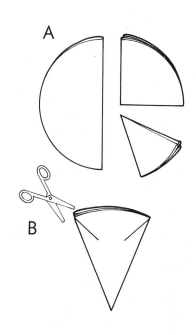

Choosing bright paper, cut a circle diameter 10cm. Fold circle in half, into a quarter and then an eighth (see Fig A). Make two diagonal cuts from each corner towards centre (see Fig B).

Unfold and lift cut section between points towards centre, tucking
last section into complete circle (see Fig C). Position a bright sticky
label in centre with the child's name and age. A paper ribbon can
be added for decoration (see photograph). Stick a piece of double
sided adhesive tape on back of badge or ribbon removing top
protective paper when placing on child.

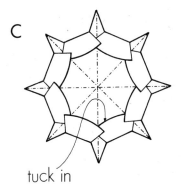

C

tuck in

Floral tribute

Flowers are frequently presented on special occasions, such as a
member of staff's retirement. If the flowers were made by the children
themselves, the gift might be particularly welcome, and indeed last
longer. The flowers shown in the photograph above are all examples
made by children (see instructions on pages 40–42). The bunch in
the vase demonstrates how different flowers look well together,
provided colours are chosen with care. The bouquet of simple square
flowers has been personalised by the addition of leaves on which the
children have written messages and signed their names.

Leaving present

This is an idea that would be particularly suitable for a member of staff who was moving from the area or about to embark on travels.

Pieces of varying coloured paper would be given to the children. Each child would draw and cut out an article of clothing or personal item that one would pack into a suitcase. (Preferably, each would choose a different object.) The front of the cut-out would be carefully decorated with pens or crayons and the back would have the signature of the child and, depending on their age, a message of farewell.
All the separate items could then be strung together with cotton or packed loose into a 'suitcase' bearing a luggage label with the name and destination of the leaving person.

If available, an old discarded suitcase could be used but, failing that, one could be made from a cardboard box or boxes. The suitcase would be as elaborate or as simple as time and resources allow.
I managed to find two shallow grocery boxes, one fitting over the other as a lid. I lined the insides with brown paper and covered the outsides with adhesive-backed plastic printed in a woven basket-work design.
If cardboard triangles are glued inside the lid at each corner (see Fig A) they would prevent the lid from totally covering the bottom box and so give a fatter suitcase. A strip of adhesive-backed plastic can be used to form the hinge of the case (see Fig B). A cardboard handle decorated with adhesive paper can be glued on to the lid. The suitcase could be completed with decorative reinforced corners (see illustration), small gold adhesive labels forming the studs.
As a final detail, someone might have fun adding 'old' travel stickers from improbable places.

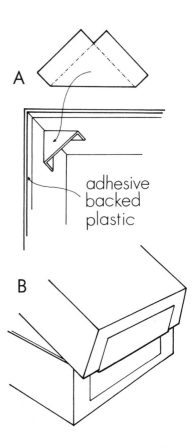

A

adhesive backed plastic

B

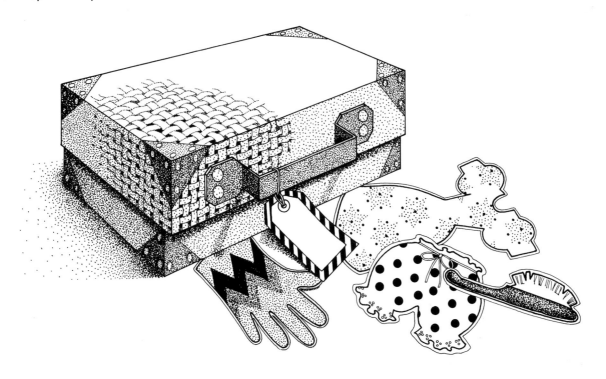

Toboggan and ski run see Page 28

For details of further Belair Publications please write to:

Belair Publications Ltd.,
P.O. Box 12,
TWICKENHAM,
TW1 2QL,
ENGLAND.